Staring at the Sun

"Irv Yalom has written a beautiful and courageous book—a book that comforts even as it explores and confronts death. Yalom helps us understand that we must all come to grips with a paradox: The physicality of death destroys us; the idea of death saves us."

George Valliant, author, *Aging Well*, and director of the Harvard Medical School Study of Adult Development

"In *Staring at the Sun*, Irv Yalom brings uncommon wisdom as a gifted psychiatrist now in his mid-seventies to a universal human experience: the terror of death. He provides a brilliant, enriching, and transforming perspective to our fears. *Staring at the Sun* is riveting, compelling, and ultimately uplifting reading. A crowning achievement."

Jack D. Barchas, M.D., chair and psychiatrist-in-chief, Weill Cornell Medical College, NewYork-Presbyterian Hospital, Payne Whitney Manhattan and Westchester

"In *Staring at the Sun*, Dr. Yalom shares with us the problems of his patients linked to their mortality, his compassionate, healing insight into their death anxiety, and perhaps most movingly, his own feelings and personal experiences with death. While the existential realities of death, isolation, and meaninglessness may seem at first bleak and full of despair, Dr. Yalom's existential approach helps his readers frame these realities in positive and meaningful ways that foster personal growth and intensify our connections to others and to the world around us."

Harold Ramis, actor, writer, and director (*Ghostbusters*, *Groundhog Day*, and *Analyze This*)

STARING AT
THE SUN

STARING AT THE SUN

Overcoming the Terror of Death

Irvin D. Yalom

Le soleil ni la mort ne se peuvent regarder en face.
(You cannot stare straight into the face of the sun, or death.)
FRANÇOIS DE LA ROCHEFOUCAULD, MAXIM 26

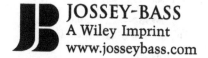
JOSSEY-BASS
A Wiley Imprint
www.josseybass.com

Published by Jossey-Bass
A Wiley Imprint
989 Market Street, San Francisco, CA 94103-1741—www.josseybass.com

The contents of this work are intended to further general scientific research, understanding,
and discussion only and are not intended and should not be relied upon as recommending or
promoting a specific method, diagnosis, or treatment by physicians for any particular patient.
The publisher and the author make no representations or warranties with respect to the
accuracy or completeness of the contents of this work and specifically disclaim all warranties,
including without limitation any implied warranties of fitness for a particular purpose. In
view of ongoing research, equipment modifications, changes in governmental regulations,
and the constant flow of information relating to the use of medicines, equipment, and
devices, the reader is urged to review and evaluate the information provided in the package
insert or instructions for each medicine, equipment, or device for, among other things, any
changes in the instructions or indication of usage and for added warnings and precautions.
Readers should consult with a specialist where appropriate. The fact that an organization
or Web site is referred to in this work as a citation and/or a potential source of further
information does not mean that the author or the publisher endorses the information the
organization or Web site may provide or recommendations it may make. Further, readers
should be aware that Internet Web sites listed in this work may have changed or disappeared
between when this work was written and when it is read. No warranty may be created
or extended by any promotional statements for this work. Neither the publisher nor
the author shall be liable for any damages arising herefrom.

Jossey-Bass books and products are available through most bookstores. To contact
Jossey-Bass directly call our Customer Care Department within the U.S.
at 800-956-7739, outside the U.S. at 317-572-3986, or fax 317-572-4002.

Jossey-Bass also publishes its books in a variety of electronic formats.
Some content that appears in print may not be available in electronic books.

The names and identities of the people in this book have been changed, and occasionally
some case composites have been made. But the essence of each story is accurate and true
to the author's experience. All the patients described have read the author's text,
collaborated on identity change, and approved these descriptions.

Library of Congress Cataloging-in-Publication Data
Yalom, Irvin D., date.
Staring at the sun : overcoming the terror of death / Irvin D. Yalom.
p. cm.
Includes bibliographical references and index.
ISBN 978-0-7879-9668-0 (cloth)
ISBN 978-0-4704-0181-1 (paperback)
1. Death—Psychological aspects. I. Title.
BF789.D4Y35   2008
155.9'37—dc22   2007027048

Printed in the United States of America
FIRST EDITION
HB Printing
PB Printing   SKY10061281_112823

Contents

Dedicated to my mentors who ripple

through me to my readers:

John Whitehorn, Jerome Frank,

David Hamburg, and Rollo May

Preface and Acknowledgments

This book is not, and cannot be, a compendium of thoughts about death, for throughout the millennia, every serious writer has addressed human mortality.

Instead, this is a deeply personal book stemming from my confrontation with death. I share the fear of death with every human being: it is our dark shadow from which we are never severed. These pages contain what I have learned about overcoming the terror of death from my own experience, my work with my patients, and the thoughts of those writers who have informed my work.

I am grateful to many who have helped along the way. My agent, Sandy Dijkstra, and my editor, Alan Rinzler, were instrumental in helping me shape and focus this book. A host of friends and colleagues have read parts of the book and offered suggestions: David Spiegel, Herbert Kotz, Jean Rose, Ruthellen Josselson, Randy Weingarten, Neil Brast, Rick Van Rheenen, Alice Van Harten, Roger Walsh, Robert Berger, and Maureen Lila. Philippe Martial introduced me to the La Rouchefoucauld maxim on the title page. My gratitude to Van Harvey, Walter Sokel, Dagfin Follesdal, my dear friends and long-term tutors in intellectual history. Phoebe Hoss and Michele Jones provided excellent editing. My four children, Eve, Reid, Victor, and Ben, were invaluable consultants, and my wife, Marilyn, as always, forced me to write better.

Most of all I am indebted to my primary teachers: my patients, who must remain unnamed (but they know who they are). They have honored me with their deepest fears, given me permission to use their stories, advised me about effective identity disguise, read some or all of the manuscript, offered advice, and taken pleasure in the thought of rippling their experience and wisdom to my readers.

STARING AT
THE SUN

Chapter 1

THE MORTAL WOUND

———

Sorrow enters my heart. I am afraid of death.
GILGAMESH

Self-awareness is a supreme gift, a treasure as precious as life. This is what makes us human. But it comes with a costly price: the wound of mortality. Our existence is forever shadowed by the knowledge that we will grow, blossom, and, inevitably, diminish and die.

Mortality has haunted us from the beginning of history. Four thousand years ago, the Babylonian hero Gilgamesh reflected on the death of his friend Enkidu with the words from the epigraph above: "Thou hast become dark and cannot hear me. When I die shall I not be like Enkidu? Sorrow enters my heart. I am afraid of death."

Gilgamesh speaks for all of us. As he feared death, so do we all—each and every man, woman, and child. For some of us the fear of death manifests only indirectly, either as generalized unrest or masqueraded as another psychological symptom; other individuals experience an explicit and conscious stream of anxiety about death; and for some of us the fear of death erupts into terror that negates all happiness and fulfillment.

For eons, thoughtful philosophers have attempted to dress the wound of mortality and to help us fashion lives of harmony and peace. As a psychotherapist treating many individuals struggling with death anxiety, I have found that ancient wisdom, particularly that of the ancient Greek philosophers, is thoroughly relevant today.

Indeed, in my work as a therapist, I take as my intellectual ancestors not so much the great psychiatrists and psychologists of the late nineteenth and early twentieth centuries—Pinel, Freud, Jung, Pavlov, Rorschach, and Skinner—but classical Greek philosophers, particularly Epicurus. The more I learn about this extraordinary Athenian thinker, the more strongly I recognize Epicurus as the proto-existential psychotherapist, and I will make use of his ideas throughout this work.

He was born in the year 341 B.C.E., shortly after the death of Plato, and died in 270 B.C.E. Most people today are familiar with his name through the word *epicure* or *epicurean,* to signify a person devoted to refined sensuous enjoyment (especially good food and drink). But in historical reality, Epicurus did not advocate sensuous pleasure; he was far more concerned with the attainment of tranquility (ataraxia).

Epicurus practiced "medical philosophy" and insisted that just as the doctor treats the body, the philosopher must treat the soul. In his view, there was only one proper goal of philosophy: to alleviate human misery. And the root cause of misery? Epicurus believed it to be *our omnipresent fear of death.* The frightening vision of inevitable death, he said, interferes with one's enjoyment of life and leaves no pleasure undisturbed. To alleviate the fear of death, he developed several powerful thought experiments that have helped me personally face death anxiety and offer the tools I use to help my patients. in the discussion that follows, I often refer to these valuable ideas.

My personal experience and clinical work have taught me that anxiety about dying waxes and wanes throughout the life cycle. Children at an early age cannot help but note the glimmerings of mortality surrounding them—dead leaves, insects and pets, disappearing grandparents, grieving parents, endless acres of cemetery tombstones. Children may simply observe, wonder, and, following their parents' example, remain silent. If they openly express their anxiety, their parents become noticeably uncomfortable and, of course, rush to offer comfort. Sometimes adults attempt to find soothing words, or transfer the whole matter into the distant future, or soothe children's anxiety with death-denying tales of resurrection, eternal life, heaven, and reunion.

The fear of death ordinarily goes underground from about six to puberty, the same years Freud designated as the period of latent sexuality. Then, during adolescence, death anxiety erupts in force: teenagers often become preoccupied with death; a few consider suicide. Many adolescents today may respond to death anxiety by becoming masters and dispensers of death in their second life in violent video games. Others defy death with gallows humor and death-taunting songs, or by watching horror films with friends. In my early adolescence I went twice a week to a small cinema around the corner from my father's store and, in concert with my friends, screamed during horror movies and gawked at the endless films depicting the barbarity of World War II. I remember shuddering silently at the sheer capriciousness of being born in 1931 rather than five years earlier like my cousin, Harry, who died in the slaughter of the Normandy invasion.

Some adolescents defy death by taking daredevil risks. One of my male patients—who had multiple phobias and a pervasive dread that something catastrophic could happen at any moment—told me how he began skydiving at the age of sixteen and took dozens of dives. Now, looking back, he believes this was a way of dealing with his persistent fear of his own mortality.

As the years go by, adolescent death concerns are pushed aside by the two major life tasks of young adulthood: pursuing a career and beginning a family. Then, three decades later, as children leave home and the end points of professional careers loom, the midlife crisis bursts upon us, and death anxiety once again erupts with great force. As we reach the crest of life and look at the path before us, we apprehend that the path no longer ascends but slopes downward toward decline and diminishment. From that point on, concerns about death are never far from mind.

It's not easy to live every moment wholly aware of death. It's like trying to stare the sun in the face: you can stand only so much of it. Because we cannot live frozen in fear, we generate methods to soften death's terror. We project ourselves into the future through our children; we grow rich, famous, ever larger; we develop compulsive protective rituals; or we embrace an impregnable belief in an ultimate rescuer.

Some people—supremely confident in their immunity—live heroically, often without regard for others or for their own safety. Still others attempt to transcend the painful separateness of death by way of merger—with a loved one, a cause, a community, a Divine Being. Death anxiety is the mother of all religions, which, in one way or another, attempt to temper the anguish of our finitude. God, as formulated transculturally, not only softens the pain of mortality through some vision of everlasting life but also palliates fearful isolation by offering an eternal presence, and provides a clear blueprint for living a meaningful life.

But despite the staunchest, most venerable defenses, we can never completely subdue death anxiety: it is always there, lurking in some hidden ravine of the mind. Perhaps, as Plato says, we cannot lie to the deepest part of ourselves.

Had I been a citizen of ancient Athens circa 300 B.C.E. (a time often called the golden age of philosophy) and experienced a death panic or a nightmare, to whom would I have turned to clear my mind of the web of fear? It's likely I'd have trudged off to the agora, a section of ancient Athens where many of the important schools of philosophy were located. I'd have walked past the Academy founded by Plato, now directed by his nephew, Speucippus; and also the Lyceum, the school of Aristotle, once a student of Plato, but too philosophically divergent to be appointed his successor. I'd have passed the schools of the Stoics and the Cynics and ignored any itinerant philosophers searching for students. Finally, I'd have reached the Garden of Epicurus, and there I think I would have found help.

Where today do people with unmanageable death anxiety turn? Some seek help from their family and friends; others turn to their church or to therapy; still others may consult a book such as this. I've worked with a great many individuals terrified by death. I believe that the observations, reflections, and interventions I've developed in a lifetime of therapeutic work can offer significant help and insight to those who cannot dispel death anxiety on their own.

In this first chapter, I want to emphasize that the fear of death creates problems that may not at first seem directly related to mortality. Death has a long reach, with an impact that is often concealed. Though fear of dying can totally immobilize some people, often the fear is covert and expressed in symptoms that appear to have nothing to do with one's mortality.

Freud believed that much psychopathology results from a person's repression of sexuality. I believe his view is far too narrow. In my clinical work, I have come to understand that one may repress not just sexuality but one's whole creaturely self and especially its finite nature.

In Chapter Two, I discuss ways of recognizing covert death anxiety. Many people have anxiety, depression, and other symptoms that are fueled by the fear of death. In this chapter, as in those to follow, I'll illustrate my points with clinical case histories and techniques from my practice as well as with stories from film and from literature.

In Chapter Three, I will show that confronting death need not result in despair that strips away all purpose in life. On the contrary, it can be an awakening experience to a fuller life. The central thesis of this chapter is: *though the physicality of death destroys us, the idea of death saves us.*

Chapter Four describes and discusses some of the powerful ideas posited by philosophers, therapists, writers, and artists for overcoming the fear of death. But, as Chapter Five suggests, ideas alone may be no match for the terror surrounding death. It is the synergy of ideas and human connection that is our most powerful aid in staring down death, and I suggest many practical ways to apply this synergy in our everyday life.

This book presents a point of view based on my observations of those who have come to me for help. But because the observer always influences what is observed, I turn in Chapter Six to an examination of the observer and offer a memoir of my personal experiences with death and my attitudes about mortality. I, too, grapple with mortality and, as a professional who has been working with death anxiety for my entire career and as a man for whom death looms closer and closer, I want to be candid and clear about my experience with death anxiety.

Chapter Seven offers instruction to therapists. For the most part, therapists avoid working directly with death anxiety. Perhaps it is because they are reluctant to face their own. But even more important is that professional schools offer little or no training in an existential approach: young therapists have told me that they don't inquire too deeply into death anxiety because they don't know what to do with the answers they receive. To be helpful to clients bedeviled by death anxiety, therapists need a new set of ideas and a new type of relationship with their patients. Although I direct this chapter toward therapists, I try to avoid professional jargon and hope the prose is clear enough for eavesdropping by any reader.

Why, you may ask, take on this unpleasant, frightening subject? Why stare into the sun? Why not follow the advice of the venerable dean of American psychiatry, Adolph Meyer, who, a century ago, cautioned psychiatrists, "Don't scratch where it doesn't itch"? Why grapple with the most terrible, the darkest and most unchangeable aspect of life? Indeed, in recent years, the advent of managed care, brief therapy, symptom control, and attempts to alter thinking patterns have only exacerbated this blinkered point of view.

Death, however, *does* itch. It itches all the time; it is always with us, scratching at some inner door, whirring softly, barely audibly, just under the membrane of consciousness. Hidden and disguised, leaking out in a variety of symptoms, it is the wellspring of many of our worries, stresses, and conflicts.

I feel strongly—as a man who will himself die one day in the not-too-distant future and as a psychiatrist who has spent decades dealing with death anxiety—that confronting death allows us, not to open some noisome Pandora's box, but to reenter life in a richer, more compassionate manner.

So I offer this book optimistically. I believe that it will help you stare death in the face and, in so doing, not only ameliorate terror but enrich your life.

Chapter 2

RECOGNIZING DEATH ANXIETY

———

Death is everything
And it is nothing.

The worms crawl in, the worms crawl out.

Each person fears death in his or her own way. For
some people, death anxiety is the background
music of life, and any activity evokes the thought that a
particular moment will never come again. Even an old
movie feels poignant to those who cannot stop thinking
that all the actors are now only dust.

For other people, the anxiety is louder, unruly,
tending to erupt at three in the morning, leaving them
gasping at the specter of death. They are besieged by
the thought that they, too, will soon be dead—as will
everyone around them.

Others are haunted by a particular fantasy of impending death: a gun pointed at their head, a Nazi firing

squad, a locomotive thundering toward them, a fall from a bridge or skyscraper.

Death scenarios take vivid forms. One person is locked in a casket, his nostrils stuffed with soil, yet conscious of lying in darkness forever. Another fears never seeing, hearing, or touching a loved one. Others feel the ache of being under the ground while all one's friends are above it. Life will go as before without the possibility of ever knowing what will happen to one's family, friends, or one's world.

Each of us has a taste of death when slipping into sleep every night or when losing consciousness under anesthesia. Death and sleep, Thanatos and Hypnos in the Greek vocabulary, were twins. The Czech existential novelist Milan Kundera suggests that we also have a foretaste of death through the act of forgetting: "What terrifies most about death is not the loss of the future but the loss of the past. In fact, the act of forgetting is a form of death always present within life."

In many people, death anxiety is overt and easily recognizable, however distressing. In others, it is subtle, covert, and hidden behind other symptoms, and it is identified only by exploration, even excavation.

OVERT DEATH ANXIETY

Many of us commingle anxiety about death with the fear of evil, abandonment, or annihilation. Others are

staggered by the enormity of eternity, of being dead forever and ever and ever and ever; others are unable to
grasp the state of nonbeing and ponder the question of
where they will be when they are dead; others focus on
the horror of their entire personal world vanishing;
others wrestle with the issue of death's inevitability, as
expressed in this e-mail from a thirty-two-year-old
woman with bouts of death anxiety:

*I suppose the strongest feelings came from realizing it
would be ME who will die, not some other entity like Old-
Lady-Me or Terminally-Ill-and-Ready-to-Die-Me. I suppose I always thought about death obliquely, as something
that* might *happen rather than* would *happen. For weeks
after a strong panic episode I thought about death more
intently than I ever had and know now it is no longer
something that* might *happen. I felt as though I had awakened to a terrible truth and could never go back.*

Some people take their fear further to an unbearable conclusion: that neither their world nor any memories of it will exist anywhere. Their street, their world of
family gatherings, parents, children, beach house, high
school, favorite camping sites—all evaporate with their
death. Nothing stable, nothing enduring. What possible
meaning can a life of such evanescence contain? The e-
mail continued:

*I became acutely aware of meaninglessness—of how every-
thing we do seems doomed to oblivion, and of the planet's*

eventual demise. I imagined the deaths of my parents, sis-
ters, boyfriend and friends. Often I think about how one
day MY skull and bones, not a hypothetical or imaginary
set of skull and bones, will be on the outside rather than the
inside of my body. That thought is very disorientating. The
idea of being an entity separate from my body doesn't really
wash with me so I can't console myself with the idea of the
imperishable soul.

There are several main themes in this young
woman's statement: death has become personalized for
her; it is no longer something that *might* happen or that
happens only to *others;* the inevitability of death makes
all life meaningless. She regards the idea of an immortal soul separate from her physical body as highly un-
likely and can find no comfort in the concept of an
afterlife. She also raises the question of whether oblivion after death is the same as oblivion before birth (an
important point that will come up again in our discussion of Epicurus).

A patient with death panics handed me this poem
at our first session:

Death pervades.
Its presence plagues me,
Grips me; drives me.
I cry out in anguish.
I carry on.

Every day annihilation looms.
I try leaving traces
That maybe matter;
Engaging in the present.
The best I can do.

But death lurks just beneath
That protective façade
Whose comfort I cling to
Like a child's blanket.
The blanket is permeable
In the stillness of the night
When the terror returns.

There will be no more self
To breathe in nature,
To right the wrongs,
To feel sweet sadness.
Unbearable loss, though
Borne without awareness.

Death is everything
And it is nothing.

She was especially haunted by the thought expressed in her last two lines: *Death is everything / And it is nothing.* She explained that the thought of becoming nothing consumed her and became everything. But the poem contains two important comforting thoughts: that by leaving traces of herself, her life will gain in meaning, and that the best she can do is to embrace the present moment.

THE FEAR OF DYING IS NOT A STAND-IN FOR SOMETHING ELSE

Psychotherapists often assume, mistakenly, that overt death anxiety is not anxiety about death, but is instead a mask for some other problem. This was the case with Jennifer, a twenty-nine-year-old realtor, whose lifelong nightly death panic attacks had not been taken at face value by previous therapists. Throughout her life, Jennifer frequently awoke during the night, sweat-drenched, eyes wide open, trembling at her own annihilation. She thought of herself vanishing, stumbling in darkness forever, entirely forgotten by the world of the living. She told herself that nothing really matters if everything is ultimately slated for utter extinction.

Such thoughts had plagued her since early childhood. She vividly recalls the first episode when she was five. Running to her parents' bedroom shaking with fear about dying, she was soothed by her mother, who told her two things she has never forgotten:

"You have a very long life ahead of you, and
it makes no sense to think of it now."

"When you're very old and approach death, then you'll be at peace or you'll be ill, and either way death won't be unwelcome."

Jennifer had relied on her mother's words of comfort all her life and had also developed additional strategies for ameliorating the attacks. She reminds herself that she has the choice whether or not to think about death. Or she tries to draw from her memory bank of good experiences—laughing with childhood friends, marveling at mirrored lakes and pillared clouds while hiking with her husband in the Rockies, kissing the sunny faces of her children.

Nevertheless, her dread of death continued to plague her and strip away much of her life contentment. She had consulted several therapists with little benefit. Various medications had diminished the intensity but not the frequency of the attacks. Her therapists never focused on her fear of death because they believed that death was a stand-in for some other anxiety. I resolved not to repeat the errors of previous therapists. I believe they had been confounded by a powerful recurrent dream that first visited Jennifer at the age of five:

My whole family is in the kitchen. There is a bowl of earthworms on the table, and my father forces me to pick up a handful, squeeze them, and then drink the milk that comes from them.

To each therapist she had consulted, the imagery of squeezing worms to obtain milk suggested, understandably, penis and semen; and each, as a result, inquired about possible sexual abuse by the father. This was my first thought also, but I discarded it after hearing Jennifer's account of how such inquiries had inevitably led to wrong directions in therapy. Although her father was extremely frightening and verbally abusive, neither she nor her siblings recalled any incidents of sexual abuse.

None of her previous therapists explored the severity and the meaning of her omnipresent fear of death. This common error has a venerable tradition, its roots stretching back to the very first publication in psychotherapy: Freud and Breuer's 1895 *Studies on Hysteria*. A careful reading of that text reveals that the fear of death pervaded the lives of Freud's patients. His failure to explore death fears would be baffling were it not for his later writings, which explain how his theory of the origins of neurosis rested on the assumption of conflict between various unconscious, primitive, instinctual forces. Death could play no role in the genesis of neurosis, Freud wrote, because it has no representation in the unconscious. He offered two reasons: first, we have no personal experience of death, and, second, it is not possible for us to contemplate our nonbeing.

Even though Freud wrote poignantly and wisely about death in such short, nonsystematic essays as "Our Attitudes Toward Death," written during the aftermath of World War I, his "de-deathification," as Robert Jay Lifton put it, of death in formal psychoanalytic theory greatly influenced generations of therapists to shift away from death and toward what they believed death represented in the unconscious, particularly abandonment and castration. Indeed, one could argue that the psychoanalytic emphasis on the past is a retreat from the future and from confrontation with death.

From the very beginning of my work with Jennifer, I embarked on an explicit exploration of her fears of death. There was no resistance: she was eager to work and had chosen to see me because she had read my text *Existential Psychotherapy* and wanted to confront the existential facts of life. Our therapy sessions concentrated on her death ideas, memories, and fantasies. I asked her to take careful notes of her dreams and her thoughts during death panics.

She didn't have long to wait. Just a few weeks later, she experienced a severe death panic after viewing a movie about the Nazi period. She was profoundly rattled by the complete capriciousness of life portrayed in the film. Innocent hostages were arbitrarily chosen and arbitrarily killed. Danger was everywhere; nowhere was safety to be found. She was struck by the similarities with her childhood home: danger from her father's unpredictable episodes of rage, her sense of having no place to hide and of seeking refuge only in invisibility—that is, by saying and asking as little as possible.

Shortly afterward, she revisited her childhood home and, as I had suggested, meditated by her parents' graves. Asking a patient to meditate by a grave may seem radical, but in 1895 Freud described giving those very instructions to a patient. When standing by her father's gravestone, Jennifer suddenly had a strange thought about him: "How cold he must be in the grave."

We discussed that odd thought. It was as if her child's view of death with its irrational components (for example, that the dead could still feel cold) was still alive in her imagination side by side with her adult rationality.

As she drove home from this session, a tune popular during her childhood crept into her mind, and she began to sing, surprised at her total recall of the lyrics:

> *Did you ever think, as a hearse goes by,*
> *That you might be the next to die?*
> *They wrap you up in a big white sheet,*
> *And bury you down about six feet deep*
> *They put you in a big black box,*
> *And cover you up with dirt and rocks,*
> *And all goes well, for about a week,*
> *And then the coffin begins to leak!*
> *The worms crawl in, the worms crawl out,*
> *The worms play pinochle on your snout.*
> *They eat your eyes, they eat your nose,*
> *They eat the jelly between your toes.*
> *A great big worm with rolling eyes,*

Crawls in your stomach and out your eyes,
Your stomach turns a slimy green,
And pus pours out like whipping cream.
You spread it on a slice of bread,
And that's what you eat when you are dead.

As she sang, memories trickled in of her sisters (Jennifer was the youngest) teasing her unmercifully by singing this song repeatedly, without regard for her obvious and palpable distress.

Recalling the song was an epiphany for Jennifer, leading her to understand that her recurrent dream about drinking the milk of earthworms was not about sex but about death, grave worms, and the danger and lack of safety she had experienced as a child. This insight—that she was keeping in suspended animation a childhood view of death—opened up new vistas for her in therapy.

COVERT DEATH ANXIETY

It may require a sleuth to bring covert death anxiety into the open, but often anyone, whether in therapy or not, can uncover it with self-reflection. Thoughts of death may seep into and permeate your dreams no matter how hidden from your conscious mind. Every nightmare is a dream in which death anxiety has escaped its corral and menaces the dreamer.

Nightmares awaken the sleeper and portray the dreamer's life at risk: running for one's life from a murderer, or falling from a great height, or hiding from a mortal threat, or actually dying or being dead.

Death often appears in dreams in symbolic form. For example, a middle-aged man with gastric problems and hypochondriacal concerns about stomach cancer dreamed of sitting on a plane with his family en route to an exotic Caribbean resort. Then, in the next frame, he found himself lying on the ground doubled up with stomach pain. He awoke in terror and instantly realized the meaning of the dream: *he had died of a stomach cancer, and life had gone on without him.*

Finally, certain life situations almost always evoke death anxiety: for example, a serious illness, the death of someone close, or a major irreversible threat to one's basic security—such as being raped, divorced, fired, or mugged. Reflection on such an event will generally result in the emergence of overt death fears.

ANXIETY ABOUT NOTHING IS REALLY ANXIETY ABOUT DEATH

Years ago, the psychologist Rollo May quipped that anxiety about nothing tries to become anxiety about something. In other words, anxiety about nothingness quickly attaches itself to a tangible object. Susan's story illustrates the usefulness of this concept when an individual has disproportionately high anxiety about some event.

Susan, a prim, efficient, middle-aged CPA, once consulted me because of conflict with her employer. We met for a few months, and she eventually left her job and started a competing, highly successful firm.

Several years later, when she phoned to request an emergency appointment, I could hardly recognize her voice. Ordinarily upbeat and self-possessed, Susan sounded tremulous and panicky. I saw her later the same day and was alarmed at her appearance: usually calm and stylishly dressed, she was disheveled and agitated, her face red, her eyes puffy from weeping, a slightly soiled bandage on her neck.

Haltingly, she related her story. George, her adult son, a responsible young man with a good job, was now in jail on drug charges. Police had stopped him for a minor traffic violation and found cocaine in his car. He tested positive and, because he was in a state-sponsored recovery program for previous DUI citations and this was his third drug-related offense, he was sentenced to a month's jail time and twelve months in a drug rehabilitation program.

Susan had not stopped crying for four days. She couldn't sleep or eat and had been unable to go to work (for the first time in twenty years). During the night she was tormented by horrendous visions of her son: guzzling from a bottle in a brown paper bag, filthy and with rotting teeth, dying in the gutter.

"He's going to die in jail," she told me, and went on to describe her exhaustion from pulling every string, trying every possible avenue, to obtain his release. She was crushed when she gazed at photos of him as a child—angelic, curly blond hair, soulful eyes—with an abundant, infinitely promising future.

Susan thought of herself as enormously resourceful. She was a self-created woman who had achieved success despite ineffectual and dissolute parents. In this situation, however, she felt totally helpless.

"Why has he done this to me?" she asked. "It's rebellion, a deliberate sabotage of my plans for him. What else could it be? Didn't I give him everything— every possible tool for success—the best education, lessons in tennis, piano, riding? And this is how he repays me? The shame of it—imagine my friends finding out!" Susan burned with envy as she thought of her friends' successful children.

The first thing I did was to remind her of things she already knew. Her vision of her son in the gutter was irrational, a matter of seeing catastrophe where there was none. I pointed out that all in all, he had made good progress: he was in a good rehab program and in private therapy with an excellent counselor. Recovery from addiction is rarely uncomplicated: relapses, often multiple relapses, are inevitable. And, of course, she knew that; she had recently returned from an entire week of family therapy at her son's recovery program. Moreover, her husband shared none of her great concerns about their son.

She also knew that her question, "Why has George done this to me?" was irrational, and she nodded in agreement when I said she had to take herself out of this picture. His relapse was not about her.

Any mother would be upset by her son's drug relapse and by the thought of him in jail, but Susan's reaction seemed excessive. I began to suspect that much of her anxiety had been displaced from some other source.

I was particularly struck by her profound sense of helplessness. She had always envisioned herself as enormously resourceful, and now that vision was shattered— there was nothing she could do for her son (except to disentangle herself from his life).

But why was George so hugely central in her life? Yes, he was her son. But it was more than that. He was *too* central. It was as if her whole life depended on his success. I discussed how, for many parents, children often represent an immortality project. That idea aroused her interest. She recognized that she had hoped to extend herself into the future through George, but she knew now that she had to let that go:

"He's not sturdy enough for the job," she said.

"Is any child sturdy enough for that?" I asked. "And what's more, George never signed up for that job—that's why his behavior, his relapse, is not about you!"

When, toward the end of the session, I inquired about the bandage on her neck, she told me that she had just had cosmetic surgery to tighten her neck. As I continued to inquire about the surgery, she grew impatient and strained to return to her son—the reason, she pointed out, for having contacted me.

But I persisted.

"Tell me more about your decision to have the surgery."

"Well, I hate what aging has done to my body— my breasts, my face, my drooping neck especially. My surgery is my birthday present to myself."

"Which birthday?"

"A capital B birthday. Number six zero. Last week."

She talked about being sixty and realizing that time was running out (and I talked about being seventy). Then I summed up:

"I feel certain that your anxiety is excessive, because part of you knows very well that relapses occur in almost every course of addiction treatment. I think some of your anxiety is coming from elsewhere and being displaced onto George."

Supported by Susan's vigorous nodding, I continued, "I think a lot of your anxiety is about yourself and not about George. It is connected to your sixtieth birthday, your awareness of your aging, and about death. It seems to me that at a deep level you must be considering some important questions: What will you do with the remainder of your life? What will provide meaning, especially now when you realize that George is not going to fill that job?"

Susan's demeanor had gradually shifted from impatience to intense interest. "I haven't done much thinking about aging and time running out. And it never came up in our previous therapy. But I'm getting your point."

At end of the hour she looked up at me: "I can't begin to imagine how your ideas are going to help me, but I will say this: *you caught my attention these last fifteen minutes.* This is the longest period of time in four days that George hasn't completely dominated my thinking."

We made another appointment for the next week at an early morning hour. She knew from our previous work that my mornings were reserved for writing and commented that I was breaking my pattern. I told her I was off schedule because I would be traveling part of the next week to attend my son's wedding.

Wanting to contribute anything that might be helpful, I added later as she was leaving, "It's my son's second marriage, Susan, and I remember going through a bad period at the time of his divorce—it's awful to feel helpless as a parent. So I know from experience how dreadful you've been feeling. The desire to help our kids is hardwired into us."

In the following two weeks, we focused much less on George and much more on her own life. Her anxiety about George dramatically diminished. His therapist had suggested (and I concurred) that it would be best for both Susan and George if they cut off contact for several weeks. She wanted to know more about fear of death and how most people handle it, and I shared with her many of my thoughts on death anxiety described in these pages. By the fourth week, she reported feeling back to normal, and we scheduled one follow-up session a few weeks later.

At this last session, when I asked what she had found most helpful in our work together, she made a clear distinction between the ideas I suggested and having a meaningful relationship with me.

"The most valuable thing," she said, "was what you told me about your son. I was very affected by your reaching out to me in that way. The other things we concentrated on—how I had displaced fears about my own life and death onto George—definitely caught my attention. I believe you were right on . . . but some of the ideas—for example, those you adapted from Epicurus—were very . . . uh . . . intellectual, and I can't tell how much they really helped. There's no question, though, that something happened in our meetings that was very effective."

The dichotomy she made between ideas and connection is a key point (see Chapter Five). However helpful ideas may be, they are vitally empowered by intimate connections with other people.

Late in that session, Susan made a startling announcement about some significant changes in her life. "One of my biggest problems is that I'm too cloistered in my work. I've been a CPA for too many years, most of my adult life, and now I've been thinking of what a bad fit that's been. I'm an extrovert in an introvert profession. I love to schmooze with people, make connections. And being a CPA is too monastic. I need to change what I do, and the last few weeks my husband and I have done some serious talking about our future. I still have time for another career. I'd hate to grow old and look back and realize I never even tried to do anything else."

She went on to tell me that she and her husband had in the past often play-talked about their dream of buying a bed-and-breakfast place in Napa Valley. Now suddenly it had gotten serious, and they had spent the previous weekend with a realtor looking at various inns for sale.

About six months later, I received a note from Susan written on the back of a photo of a charming Napa Valley country inn, urging me to come to visit. "First night on the house!"

The story of Susan illustrates several points. First, her disproportionate amount of anxiety. *Of course,* she was distressed by her child's being in jail. What parent would not be? But she was responding catastrophically. After all, her son had been having difficulties with drugs for many years and had had other relapses.

I took an educated guess when I zeroed in on the soiled bandage on her neck, the evidence of her cosmetic surgery. However, the risk for error was small, for no one in her age bracket escapes concern about aging. Her cosmetic surgery and the "marker" of her sixtieth birthday had stirred up much covert death anxiety, which she had displaced onto her son. In our therapy, I made her aware of the source of her anxiety and tried to help her confront it.

Susan was jolted by several insights: that her body was aging, that her son represented her immortality project, and that she had only limited power to help her son or to halt her aging. Ultimately her realization that she was accumulating a mountain of regret in her life initiated a major life shift.

This is the first of many examples I shall offer which demonstrate that we can do more than merely reduce death anxiety. Death awareness may serve as an awakening experience, a profoundly useful catalyst for major life changes.

Chapter 3

THE AWAKENING EXPERIENCE

One of the best known characters in literature is Ebenezer Scrooge, the grasping, isolated, mean-spirited old man in Charles Dickens's *A Christmas Carol.* Yet something happened to Ebenezer Scrooge at the end of the story—a remarkable transformation. His icy countenance melts, and he becomes warm, generous, and eager to help his employees and associates.

What happened? What fueled Scrooge's transformation? Not his conscience. Not the warmth of Yule cheer. Instead, it was a form of existential shock therapy or, as I shall refer to it in this book, an *awakening experience.* The Ghost of the Future (the Ghost of Christmas Yet to Come) visits Scrooge and delivers a powerful dose of shock therapy by offering him a preview of the future. Scrooge observes his neglected corpse, sees strangers pawning his belongings (even his bed sheets and nightdress), and overhears members of his community discuss his death and dismiss it lightly. Next, the Ghost of the Future escorts Scrooge to the churchyard to view his grave. Scrooge gazes at his tombstone, fingers the letters of his name, and at that moment *he undergoes a transformation.* In the next scene Scrooge is a new and compassionate person.

Other examples of awakening experiences—a confrontation with death that enriches life—abound in great literature and film. Pierre, the protagonist of Tolstoy's epic novel *War and Peace,* faces death by firing squad, only to be reprieved after several men in line ahead of him have been shot. A lost soul before this event, Pierre is transformed and lives with zest and purpose in the remainder of the novel. (In real life, twenty-one-year-old Dostoevsky was similarly reprieved at the last moment, and his life similarly transformed.)

Earlier thinkers, long before Tolstoy—since the beginning of the written word—have reminded us of the interdependence of life and death. The Stoics (for example, Chrysippus, Zeno, Cicero, and Marcus Aurelius) taught us that learning to live well is learning to die well and that, conversely, learning to die well is learning to live well. Cicero said that "to philosophize is to prepare for death." St. Augustine wrote, "it is only in the face of death that a man's self is born." Many medieval monks kept a human skull in their cell to focus their thoughts on mortality and its lesson for the conduct of life. Montaigne suggested that a writing studio have a good view of the cemetery in order to sharpen one's thinking. In these ways and in many others, great teachers down through the ages have reminded us that although the *physicality of death destroys us, the idea of death saves us.*

Although the physicality of death destroys us, the idea of death saves us. Let's examine that thought more closely. Saves us? From what? And *how* does the idea of death save us?

THE DIFFERENCE BETWEEN "HOW THINGS ARE" AND "THAT THINGS ARE"

A dialectic expressed by Heidegger, the twentieth-century German philosopher, clarifies this paradox. He proposed two modes of existence: the *everyday* mode and the *ontological* mode (from *onto,* "being," and the suffix *-logy,* "study of"). In your *everyday* mode, you are entirely absorbed in your surroundings, and you marvel at **how *things are*** in the world; whereas in the *ontological* mode, you focus on and appreciate the miracle of "being" itself and marvel **that *things are,* *that* you are.**

There is a crucial difference between *how* things are and *that* things are. When absorbed in the everyday mode, you turn toward such evanescent distractions as physical appearance, style, possessions, or prestige. In the ontological mode, by contrast, you are not only more aware of existence and mortality and life's other immutable characteristics but also more anxious and *more primed to make significant changes.* You are prompted to grapple with your fundamental human responsibility to construct an authentic life of engagement, connectivity, meaning, and self-fulfillment.

Many reports of dramatic and lasting changes catalyzed by a confrontation with death support this view. While working intensively over a ten-year period with patients facing death from cancer, I found that many of them, rather than succumb to numbing despair, were positively and dramatically transformed. They rearranged their life priorities by trivializing life's trivia. They assumed the power to choose *not* to do the things that they really did not wish to do. They communicated more deeply with those they loved, and appreciated more keenly the elemental facts of life—the changing seasons, the beauty of nature, the last Christmas or New Year.

Many reported a diminishment of their fears of other people, a greater willingness to take risks, and less concern about rejection. One of my patients commented drolly that "cancer cures psychoneuroses"; another said to me, "What a pity I had to wait till now, till my body was riddled with cancer, to learn how to live!"

AWAKENING AT THE END OF LIFE: TOLSTOY'S IVAN ILYCH

In Tolstoy's *The Death of Ivan Ilych,* the protagonist—a middle-aged, self-absorbed, arrogant bureaucrat—develops a fatal abdominal illness and is dying in unremitting pain. As death approaches, Ivan Ilych realizes that all his life he has shielded himself from the notion of death through his preoccupation with prestige, appearance, and money. He becomes enraged with everyone about him who perpetuates denial and falsity by offering unfounded hopes for recovery.

Then, following an astounding conversation with the deepest part of himself, he awakens in a moment of great clarity to the fact that *he is dying so badly because he has lived so badly.* His whole life has been wrong. In shielding himself from death, he had shielded himself from life as well. He compares his life to the experience he had often had in railway carriages when he thought he was going forward, but was in reality rolling backward. In short, he becomes *mindful of being.*

As fast as death approaches for Ivan Ilych, he finds there is still time. He grows aware that not only he but all living things must die. He discovers compassion—a new feeling in himself. He feels a tenderness for others: for his young son kissing his hand; for the servant boy who nurses him in a natural, loving manner; and even, for the first time, for his young wife. He feels pity for them, for the suffering he has inflicted, and ultimately dies not in pain but in the joy of intense compassion.

Tolstoy's story is not only a literary masterpiece but also a powerful instructive lesson and, indeed, is often required reading for those being trained to offer comfort to the dying.

If such a mindfulness of being is conducive to important personal change, then *how do you move out of the mode of everydayness into the more change-conducive mode?* Not from simply wishing it or bearing down and gritting your teeth. Instead, it usually takes an urgent or irreversible experience to awaken a person and jerk him or her out of the everyday mode into the ontological one. This is what I call the awakening experience.

But where are the awakening experiences for us in our everyday life, for those of us not facing terminal cancer, a firing squad, or a visit from the Ghost of the Future? In my experience, the major catalysts for an awakening experience are urgent life events:

> Grief at the loss of someone you love
> Life-threatening illness
> The breakup of an intimate relationship
> Some major life milestone, such as a big birthday
>   (fifty, sixty, seventy, and so on)
> Cataclysmic trauma, such as a fire, rape,
>   or robbery
> Children's leaving home (the empty nest)

Loss of a job or a career change
Retirement
Move to a retirement home
Finally, powerful dreams that convey a message
   from your deeper self can serve as awakening
   experiences.

Each of the following stories, drawn from my clinical practice, illustrates a different form of awakening experience. All the tactics I use with my patients are accessible to anyone: you can modify each and use it not only in your own self-inquiry but in offering help to those you love.

GRIEF AS AN AWAKENING EXPERIENCE

Grief and loss may awaken one and make one mindful of one's being—as they did for Alice, a new widow who had to deal with both grief and a move to a retirement home; for Julia, whose grief at a friend's death uncovered her own death anxiety; and for James, who buried the pain of his brother's death for years.

Transiency Forever: Alice

I was Alice's therapist for a very long time. How long? Hold on to your chairs, all of you younger readers

familiar with the contemporary brief therapy model. I
saw her for over thirty years!

Not thirty consecutive years (although I want to go
on record as saying that some people *do* require that
amount of ongoing support). Alice—who, with her
husband, Albert, owned and operated a musical instrument store—first called me when she was fifty because
of escalating conflicts with her son as well as with several friends and customers. We met in individual therapy for two years and then in a therapy group for three
years. Although she improved a great deal, several
times in the next twenty-five years she returned to therapy to deal with significant life crises. My final visit
with her took place at her bedside shortly before her
death at the age of eighty-four. Alice taught me a great
deal, especially about stressful stages during the second
half of life.

The following episode occurred during the last
course of therapy, which began when she was seventy-
five and lasted for four years. Alice called for help when
her husband was diagnosed with Alzheimer's disease.
She needed support: there are few ordeals more night-
marish than witnessing the gradual but relentless crum-
bling of the mind of a life partner.

Alice suffered as her husband passed through all
the inexorable stages: first, the radical short-term memory loss, with missing keys and wallets; then his forgetting where his automobile was parked and her cruising
the city in search of the lost vehicle; then his wandering

stage, requiring an escort home by the police; then deterioration of his personal hygiene habits; then a drastic self-absorption accompanied by loss of empathy. The final horror for Alice was when her husband of fifty-five years no longer recognized her.

After Albert died, we turned our attention to mourning and particularly to the tension she felt between grief and relief—her grief at losing the Albert she had known and loved since she was a teenager, and her relief at being released from the heavy burden of full-time care for the stranger he had become.

A few days after the funeral, after her friends and family had returned to their own full lives and she faced an empty house, a new fear arose: she grew terrified that an intruder might break into her home during the night. Nothing external had changed; her middle-class neighborhood was as stable and safe as ever. Friendly familiar neighbors, one of them a policeman, dwelled on her block. Perhaps Alice felt unprotected in the absence of her husband; even though he had been physically incapacitated for years, his mere presence provided a sense of security. Ultimately, a dream allowed her to understand the source of her terror.

I am sitting at the edge of a pool with my legs in the water, and I begin to feel creepy because there are large leaves coming toward me under the water. I can feel them brushing against my leg—ughh . . . even now the thought of them makes me feel creepy. They are black and large and ovoid. I try to move my feet to make waves which would push the leaves back, but my feet are weighed down by sandbags. Or maybe it is bags of lime.

"That's when I panicked," she said, "and woke up yelling. For hours, I avoided going back to sleep lest I return to the dream."

One of her associations to the dream illuminated its meaning.

"Bags of lime? What does that mean to you?" I asked.

"Burial," she replied. "Wasn't it lime they threw into the mass graves in Iraq? And also in London during the black plague?"

So the intruder was death. Her death. Her husband's death had left her exposed to death.

"If he can die," she said, "then so can I. So will I."

Several months after her husband's death, Alice decided to move from her house of forty years into a retirement home that offered the care and medical backup required by her severe hypertension and limited vision from macular degeneration.

Now Alice grew preoccupied with the disposition of her possessions. There was room for nothing else in her mind. Moving to a small apartment from a large four-bedroom house packed with furniture, mementos, and a collection of antique musical instruments meant, of course, that she had to dispose of a great many belongings. Her one child, a peripatetic son who now worked in Denmark and lived in a small apartment, had no room for any of her belongings. Of the painful choices she had to make, the hardest was what to do with the musical instruments she and Albert had collected over their life together. Often in the stillness and loneliness of her shrinking life she could hear the ghostly chords of her grandfather playing the Paolo Testore 1751 cello, or of her husband at the 1775 British harpsichord he loved. And then there was the English concertina and recorder that her parents had given them for a wedding present.

Every item in her household contained memories of which she was now the sole possessor. She told me that every item would be dispersed to strangers who would never know their history or cherish them as she had. And eventually her own death would finally erase all the rich memories embedded in harpsichord, cello, flutes, penny whistles, and so much else. Her past would perish with her.

The day of Alice's move loomed ominously. Bit by bit the furniture and goods she could not keep disappeared—sold, given away to friends and strangers. As her house emptied, her sense of panicky dislocation increased.

Particularly jolting was her last day in her home. Because the new owners planned extensive remodeling, they insisted the house be left entirely empty. Even

bookshelves had to be removed. As Alice watched them
being torn from the wall, she was startled to see underlying strips of robin's-egg blue paint on the wall.

Robin's-egg blue! Alice remembered this color.
Forty years before, when she first moved into her house,
the walls had been robin's-egg blue. And, for the first
time in all those years, she recalled the countenance of
the woman who had sold her the house, the pinched
face of an anguished, bitter widow who, like her, hated
to leave her home. Now Alice was also a widow, also
bitter, also hating to leave her home.

Life is a passing parade, she said to herself. Of
course! She had always known about transiency.
Hadn't she once attended a weeklong meditation workshop where the Pali word for transiency, *anicca,* was
chanted interminably? But in this, as in all things, there
is a huge difference between knowing *about* something
and knowing it through your own experience.

Now she truly realized that she too was transient,
simply passing through the house as had all its other
former occupants. And the house also was transient and
would some day pass away to make room for another
house on the same land. The process of giving up her
possessions and moving was an awakening experience
for Alice, who had always cloaked herself in the warm,
comfortable illusion of a richly furnished and tapestried
life. Now she learned that the lushness of possessions
had sheltered her from the starkness of existence.

At our next session, I read aloud to her a relevant passage from Tolstoy's *Anna Karenina* in which Anna's husband, Alexey Alexandrovitch, has realized that his wife, Anna, is truly going to leave him: "Now he experienced a feeling akin to a man who, while calmly crossing a bridge, should suddenly discover that the bridge is broken, and that there is a chasm below. That chasm was life itself, the bridge that artificial life in which Alexey Alexandrovitch had lived."

Alice, too, had a glimpse of the bare scaffolding of life and the nothingness below. The Tolstoy quotation helped Alice, partly because her experience was named and thereby imbued with a sense of familiarity and control, and partly because of its implications for our relationship—namely, my having taken the time and effort to locate the passage containing some of my favorite Tolstoy lines.

Alice's story introduces several ideas that will resurface in other vignettes in this book. Her husband's death resulted in the appearance of her own death anxiety. First it was externalized and transformed into the fear of an intruder; then it came as a nightmare; then more overtly, in the work of mourning, with the realization that "If he can die, so will I." All these experiences, plus the loss of many treasured, memory-laden possessions, shifted her into an ontological mode, which ultimately led to significant personal change.

Alice's parents were long dead, and the death of her lifetime companion confronted her with the precariousness of her existence. Now no one stood between her and the grave. This experience is by no means unusual. As I shall emphasize several times in these pages, a common but often unappreciated part of mourning is the survivor's personal confrontation with his or her own death.

An unexpected coda. When the time came for Alice to leave home and move into the retirement community, I braced myself: I worried about her falling into deeper, perhaps irrevocable, despair. Yet two days after the move, she entered my office with a lighter, almost frisky stride, sat down, and astonished me.

"I'm happy!" she said.

In all the years I had been seeing her, she had never begun a session in such a manner. What were the reasons for this euphoria? (I always teach my students that understanding the factors that make clients feel better is as important as understanding those that make them feel worse.)

Her happiness had its source in her deep past. She had grown up in foster homes, had always shared rooms with other children, had married young and moved into her husband's home, and all her life had yearned for a room of her own. Back in her teens, she had been profoundly moved by Virginia Woolf's *A Room of One's Own*. What was now making her happy, she told me, was that finally, at the age of eighty in a retirement home, she had a room of her own.

Not only that, but she felt she had an opportunity to repeat a certain part of her early life—to be single, alone, on her own—and, this time, get it right: she could allow herself, finally, to be free and autonomous. Only someone intimately connected to her and fully knowledgeable about both her past and her great unconscious complex can understand this outcome, in which the personal-unconscious-historical trumps existential concerns.

Another factor played a role in her sense of well-being: a sense of liberation. Letting her furniture go was a great loss, but also a relief. Her many belongings were precious but heavy with the weight of memory. Leaving them felt like shedding a cocoon; and, freed from the ghosts and debris of the past, she had a new room, a new skin, a new start. A new life at the age of eighty.

Death Anxiety Disguised: Julia

Julia, a forty-nine-year-old British therapist now living in Massachusetts, asked to see me for a few sessions during a two-week California visit to help her with a problem that had resisted previous therapy.

Following the death two years earlier of a close friend, Julia had not only failed to recover from her loss but also developed a set of symptoms that seriously interfered with her life. She had grown highly hypochondriacal: any slight body ache or twitch evoked alarm and precipitated a call to her physician. Moreover, she had become too fearful to pursue many of her former activities—ice skating, skiing, snorkeling— or any other that was the slightest bit risky. She had even grown uncomfortable driving and needed to take Valium before boarding the plane to California. It seemed apparent that the death of her friend had ignited considerable, thinly disguised death anxiety.

Proceeding to take a history of her ideas about death in a straightforward, matter-of-fact manner, I learned that, like many of us, she first encountered death when, as a child, she discovered dead birds and insects and attended funerals of grandparents. She had no memory of her first realization of her own inevitable death, but recalled that in adolescence she had once or twice allowed herself to think of her own death: "it was like having a trap door opening beneath me and then falling forever into blackness. I guess I made a point of not going there again."

"Julia," I then said, "let me ask you a simplistic question. Why is death so terrifying? What specifically is it about death that frightens you?"

She answered instantly, "All the things I would not have done."

"How so?"

"I'll need to tell you about my history as an artist. My first identity was as an artist. Everyone, all my teachers, let me know that I was highly talented. But, though I won considerable acclaim during my youth and adolescence, once I decided on psychology I put my art away."

Then she corrected herself, "No, that's not entirely right. I haven't entirely put it away. I often begin drawings or paintings, but I never finish them. I begin something and then shove it in my desk, which along with my closet at work is crammed with unfinished work."

"Why? If you love to paint and you begin projects, what keeps you from finishing them?"

"Money. I am very busy and have a full therapy practice."

"How much money do you earn? How much do you need?"

"Well, most people would consider it quite a bit— I see patients at least forty hours a week, often more. But there's the sky-high tuition for two children in private school."

"And your husband? You said he too is a therapist. Does he work as hard and earn as much?"

"He sees the same number of patients, sometimes more, and he earns more—a lot of his hours are neuropsych testing, which is more profitable."

"So it seems that between you and your husband you have more money than you need. Yet you tell me that money stops you entirely from pursuing your art?"

"Well, it *is* money, but in a strange sort of way. You see, my husband and I have always been in competition to see who can earn the most. It's not openly acknowledged, it's not explicit competition, but I know it's there all the time."

"Well, let me ask you a question. Let's suppose that a client came into your office and told you she was vastly talented and ached to express herself creatively, but could not do so because she was in competition with her husband to earn more money—money she did not need. What would you say to her?"

I can still hear Julia's immediate reply, her clipped British accent. "I'd say to her, *you are living a life of absurdity!*"

Julia's work in therapy, then, consisted of finding a way to live less absurdly. We explored the competitiveness in her marital relationship and also the meaning of all the half-finished drawings in her desk and closets. We considered, for example, whether the idea of an alternative destiny was acting to counteract somehow the straight line stretching from birth to death. Or could there be a payoff in her not finishing works and, thereby, not testing the limits of her talent? Perhaps she wanted to perpetuate the belief that she could have done great things if only she had wished. Perhaps there was something attractive in the idea that if she had wanted, she might have been a great artist. Perhaps no artistic piece quite reached the level she demanded of herself.

Julia especially resonated with the last thought. She was eternally dissatisfied with herself and drove herself on with a motto she had memorized from a school blackboard at the age of eight:

Good better best
Never let it rest
Until the good is better
And the better is best

Julia's story is another example of the way death anxiety may manifest itself covertly. She appeared for therapy with an array of symptoms that were a gosamer-thin disguise for death anxiety. Moreover, as in Alice's case, the symptoms arose after the death of someone close to her, an event that served as an awakening experience confronting her with her own death. Therapy moved quickly; in only a few sessions, her grief and her fearful behavior resolved, and she grappled directly with the unfulfilling way she was living her life.

"What precisely do you fear about death?", a question I often ask clients, elicits varied answers that often accelerate the work of therapy. Julia's answer, "All the things I would not have not done," points to a theme of great importance to many who ponder or face death: the *positive correlation between the fear of death and the sense of unlived life.*

In other words, the more unlived your life, the greater your death anxiety. The more you fail to experience your life fully, the more you will fear death. Nietzsche expressed this idea forcefully in two short epigrams: "Consummate your life" and "Die at the right time"—as did Zorba the Greek in urging, "Leave death nothing but a burned out castle," and Sartre, in his autobiography: "I was going quietly to my end . . . certain that the last burst of my heart would be inscribed on the last page of my work and that death would be taking only a dead man."

The Long Shadow of a Brother's Death: James

James, a forty-six-year-old paralegal, entered therapy for a number of reasons: he hated his occupation, felt restless and rootless, used alcohol excessively, and had no intimate connections aside from a troubled relationship with his wife. In our first sessions, I could discern, among a plethora of problems—interpersonal, occupational, marital, alcohol abuse—no evident concern with such existential problems as transience or mortality.

Soon, however, issues from deeper levels surfaced. For one thing, I noted that whenever we explored his isolation from others, we always seemed to end up in the same spot: his older brother Eduardo's death. Eduardo was killed at the age of eighteen in an auto accident when James was sixteen. Two years later, James left Mexico to attend college in the United States and since then saw his family only once a year: he always flew home to Oaxaca every November in remembrance of his brother at the celebration of *el día de los muertos,* the day of the dead.

Something else soon began to emerge in almost every session: the topic of origins and endings. James was consumed by eschatology, matters pertaining to the end of the world, and had practically memorized the Book of Revelations. And origins, too, fascinated him, especially ancient Sumerian texts, which in his view suggested extraterrestrial origins of humankind.

I found it difficult to deal with these topics. For one thing, his grief for his brother was not accessible: there was a great deal of amnesia surrounding his emotional response to his brother's death. Eduardo's funeral? James could recall only one thing: that he was the only one not weeping. He responded, he said, as though he were reading about some other family in the daily newspaper. Even at the annual celebration for the dead, James felt that his body was there, but neither his mind nor his spirit.

Anxiety about death? Not an issue for James, who said he found death unthreatening. In fact, he considered it a positive event and looked forward with pleasure to a reunion with his family.

I explored his paranormal beliefs from a number of directions, trying my best not to show my extreme skepticism or arouse his defensiveness. My strategy was to avoid the content (that is, the pros and cons of extraterrestrial sightings or UFO relics) and to focus instead on two things: the psychological meaning of his interest, and his epistemology—that is, how he knew what he knew (what sources he used and what constituted sufficient evidence).

I wondered aloud why he, despite an excellent education at an Ivy League college, persistently ignored scholarly research on such subjects as the origins of human beings. What was the positive payoff for him in embracing esoteric, supernatural beliefs? To my eye, they were toxic for him: they increased his isolation because he dared not share them with friends lest they dismiss him as bizarre.

All my efforts had little effect, and therapy soon stagnated. He was restless during our sessions and impatient with therapy, generally beginning each session with skeptical or flippant questions, such as "How much longer is therapy going to take, Doc? or "Am I almost cured?" or "Is this going to be one of those never-ending cases that keeps the cash register ringing?"

Then at one session he brought in a powerful dream that changed everything. Although he dreamed it several days before the session, it remained fixed in his mind with preternatural lucidity:

I am at a funeral. Someone is lying on the table. The minister is preaching about embalming techniques. People file past the body. I am in line, and I know the body had had much embalming and cosmetic work done. I steel myself and move up with the line. My gaze is first at the feet, then the legs, and I continue to sweep my eyes up. The right hand is bandaged. Then I glance at the head and know it is Eduardo, my brother. I choke up and start to cry. I have two feelings: first the sadness and then comfort because his face is undamaged and he has a good tan. "Eduardo looks good," I say to myself. And when I get to his head I lean over and say to him "You look good, Eduardo." Then I take a seat next to my sister and turn to her and say, "He looks good!" At the end of the dream I sit alone in Eduardo's room and start to read his book about the Rosewell UFO sightings.

Although he had no spontaneous associations to the dream, I urged him to "free associate" to the images. "Look at the image persisting in your mind's eye," I said, "and try to think out loud. Just describe the thoughts floating through your mind. Try not to omit or censor anything, even things that seem silly or irrelevant."

"I see a torso with hoses running in and out. I see a body lying in a pool of yellow liquid—probably embalming fluid. Nothing else comes."

"Did you, in reality, view Eduardo's body at the funeral?"

"I don't remember. I think it was a closed casket service because Eduardo was so mutilated by the accident."

"James, I see on your face so many grimaces, so many changing expressions as you think about this dream."

"It's a strange experience. On the one hand, I feel I don't want to go farther, and my concentration keeps fading. But, on the other hand, I'm drawn to the dream. It has power."

I felt the dream was so important that I persisted. "What do you think of your saying, 'Eduardo looks good'? You repeated that three times."

"Well, he *did* look good. Tanned, healthy."

"But, James, he was dead. What does it mean if a dead person looks healthy?"

"I don't know. What do *you* think?"

"I think," I responded, "his looking good was a reflection of how very much you want him to be still alive."

"My brain tells me you're right. But words are only words. I just don't feel it."

"A sixteen-year-old losing his older brother like that. Mutilated in an accident. I think it has marked your entire life. Maybe it's time for you to start feeling some sympathy for that sixteen-year-old boy."

James nodded slowly.

"You look sad, James. What are you thinking?"

"I'm remembering the phone call when my mother was told of Eduardo's accident. I listened for a moment, knew something big was wrong, and walked into the other room. I guess I didn't want to hear it."

"Not listening and not hearing is what you've done with your pain. And your denying, your drinking, your restlessness—none of it is working anymore. The pain is there; when you close one door on it, it knocks to come in somewhere else—in this instance it pours into a dream."

As James nodded, I added, "And what about the ending of the dream, that book about UFOs and Rosewell?"

James exhaled loudly and stared at the ceiling. "I knew it. I knew you were going to ask about that!"

"It's your dream, James. You created it, and you put Rosewell and the UFOs there. What's their connection with death? What comes to mind?"

"It's hard to admit this to you, but I did discover that book in my brother's bookcase and did read it after the funeral. I can't quite explain it, but it's something like this: if I could find out exactly where we came from— and maybe it *is* from UFOs and extraterrestrials—then I would live a lot better. I'd know why we're put here on this earth."

It seemed to me that he was trying to keep his brother alive by inhabiting his brother's belief system, but I doubted that this thought would be useful to him and kept my silence.

This dream and our discussion of it signaled a change in therapy. He began to take his life, and his therapy, far more seriously, and our therapeutic alliance grew stronger. I heard no more quips about my cash register and no questions about how long therapy would take or whether he was cured yet. James knew now that death had deeply marked his youth, that his grief for his brother had influenced many of his life choices, and finally that his intense pain had discouraged him from examining himself and his own mortality throughout his life.

Though he never lost interest in the paranormal, he made far-reaching changes in himself: he stopped drinking cold turkey (without reliance on a recovery program), vastly improved his relationship with his wife, quit his job, and entered the business of training seeing-eye dogs—a profession that offered meaning by providing something useful to the world.

A Major Decision as an Awakening Experience

Major decisions often have deep roots. Every choice involves a relinquishment, and each relinquishment makes us aware of limitations and temporality.

Pinned and Pinned Down: Pat

Pat, a forty-five-year-old stockbroker, divorced for four years, sought therapy because of difficulty in establishing a new relationship. I had seen her for several months five years before when she decided to leave her marriage. Her reason for contacting me again was that she had met an attractive new man, Sam, who interested her but had unleashed a storm of anxiety.

Pat told me she was enmeshed in a paradox: she loved Sam, but was tormented about continuing to see him. The final straw prompting her to phone me was that she had received an invitation to a party to be attended by many of her close friends and business associates. Should she or should she not bring Sam? This dilemma loomed larger and larger until she obsessed about it nonstop.

Why such turmoil? In our first session, after unsuccessful attempts to help her reason through the meaning of her discomfort, I tried an indirect approach and suggested a guided fantasy.

"Pat, try this; I think it will help. I want you to close your eyes and imagine Sam and you arriving at the party. You enter the room holding hands with him. Many of your friends see you; they wave and walk toward you." I paused. "You see that in your mind's eye?"

She nodded.

"Now keep looking at that scene and let your feelings seep in. Check into yourself and tell me everything you feel. Try to be loose. Say everything that comes to mind."

"Ugh, the party. Don't like it." She winced. "I let go of Sam's hand. I don't want to be seen with him."

"Keep going. Why not?"

"Don't know why! He's older than I am, but only two years. And he's a great-looking guy. He works in PR, and he knows how to handle himself socially. But I, or we, would be labeled as a couple. An older couple. I'd be pinned down. Limited. I'd be saying no to every other man. 'Pinned' and 'pinned down'"—she opened her eyes—"you know, I never thought of that double meaning before. Like in college when you're wearing some guy's fraternity pin, you're pinned to him, but you're also pinned down."

"What an apt way to depict your dilemma, Pat. Other feelings?"

Pat closed her eyes again and sank back into her fantasy. "There's stuff about my marriage coming up. I feel guilty about having wrecked my marriage. I know from our previous therapy that I didn't wreck it—you and I worked hard on that guilt—but damned if the idea is not creeping back now. My failed marriage was my first real-life failure—everything was progressing upward before that. Of course, the marriage is over. Over for years. But actually choosing another man makes the divorce real. It signifies I cannot go back— ever. It's a past stage of my life. It's irreversible . . . a vanished time. Yes, yes, I've known this, but not like I suddenly know it now."

Pat's story illustrates the relationship between freedom and mortality. Difficult decisions often have roots that reach into the bedrock of existential concerns and personal responsibility. Let's examine why Pat's decision was so agonizing.

For one thing, it portended relinquishment. Every yes involves a no. Once she gets "pinned" to Sam, other

possibilities—other younger, perhaps superior men—
are ruled out. As she put it, she would not only be
pinned to Sam but pinned down. She would be cutting
off other possibilities. That narrowing of possibilities
has a dark side: the more possibilities you close off, the
smaller, shorter, and less vital your life appears.

Heidegger once defined death as "the impossibility
of further possibility." So Pat's anxiety—ostensibly
about a superficial thing, a decision about taking a man
to a party—drew its power from the bottomless well of
her death anxiety. It served as an awakening experience: our focus on the deeper meaning of her decision
sharply increased the effectiveness of our work.

Our analysis of responsibility led her to a greater
realization of the impossibility of returning to youth.
She also mentioned that her life had seemed to be progressing upward until the divorce, but now realized
that the divorce was truly irreversible. Eventually, she
let it go, accepted the relinquishment, turned to the
future, and was able to make a commitment to Sam.

Pat's illusion that we are ever growing, progressing,
moving upward is not uncommon. It has been greatly
reinforced by Western civilization's idea of progress
existing since the Enlightenment, and by the American
imperative for upward mobility. Of course, progress is
merely a construct; there are other ways to conceptualize
history. The ancient Greeks did not subscribe to the idea
of progress: on the contrary, they looked backward
toward a golden age that blazed more brightly with the

passing centuries. The sudden realization that upward progress is but a myth can be jolting, as it was for Pat, and entails considerable shifting of ideas and beliefs.

LIFE MILESTONES AS AWAKENING EXPERIENCES

Other instances of awakening—both more ordinary and more subtle—are associated with such milestones in life as school and college reunions; birthdays and anniversaries; estate planning and making a will; and major birthdays, such as the fiftieth or sixtieth.

School and College Reunions

School and college reunions, especially after twenty-five years, are potentially rich experiences. Nothing makes the life cycle more palpable than to see your classmates now all grown up and indeed aged. And of course the roll call of classmates who have died is an ever more sobering and powerful wake-up call. Some reunions supply pictures of the young faces to pin on lapels, and participants circulate around the room comparing photographs and faces, trying to find the young, innocent eyes in the wrinkled masks before them. And who can resist thinking: "So old, they're all so old. What am I doing in this group? What must I look like to them?"

For me a reunion is like the conclusion to stories that I began reading thirty, forty, even fifty years before. Classmates have a shared history, a sense of deep intimacy with one another. They knew you when you were young and fresh and before you had developed a grown-up persona. Perhaps this is the reason that reunions give rise to an astonishing number of new marriages. Old classmates feel trustworthy, old loves are rekindled, all are members of a drama begun long ago against a backdrop of limitless hope. I encourage my patients to attend their reunions and to keep a journal of their reactions when they do.

Estate Planning

Estate planning inevitably raises existential awareness as you discuss your death and your heirs and ponder the disposition of the money and goods you have accumulated throughout your lifetime. This process of summarizing your life raises many questions: Whom do I love? Whom don't I love? Who will miss me? To whom should I be generous? In this time of reviewing your life, you have to take practical measures to face its end, to make burial arrangements, to confront and resolve unfinished business.

One of my clients with a fatal illness, who began the process of putting his affairs in order, spent days going through his e-mail to eliminate all messages that might cause discomfort to his family. As he deleted mail from old lovers, he was suffused with pathos. The final obliteration of all photos and mementos, of soaring passionate experiences, inevitably evokes existential anxiety.

Birthdays and Anniversaries

Significant birthdays and anniversaries can also be potential awakening experiences. Although generally we celebrate birthdays with gifts, cakes, cards, and joyous parties, what is the celebration really about? Perhaps it is an attempt to dispel any sad reminder of the inexorable rush of time. Therapists do well to take note of patients' birthdays—especially significant ones, the big decade anniversaries—and inquire about the feelings they evoke.

TURNING FIFTY: WILL Any therapist who has attained a sensitivity to mortal issues will be impressed by their ubiquity. Again and again, I have started to write a section of this book only to have, on that very day, a patient drop a relevant clinical illustration into my lap without my having consciously pulled for it. Consider this therapy hour occurring as I wrote this chapter on awakening experiences.

It was my fourth meeting with Will, an exceedingly cerebral forty-nine-year-old attorney, seeking therapy because he had lost his passion for work and was dismayed that he had not put his own considerable intellectual gifts to the best use. (He had graduated magna cum laude from an outstanding university.)

Will began the session by commenting that some of his coworkers were openly critical of his doing excessive pro bono work and having too few billable hours. After fifteen minutes describing his work situation, he discussed at length his history of always having been a misfit in organizations. It seemed important background information, and I took it all in, but I remained mostly silent in this part of the session—aside from commenting on the compassion he showed in describing his pro bono cases.

After a brief silence he said, "By the way, today is my fiftieth birthday."

"And? How does that feel?"

"Well, my wife's going to make a fuss over it. She's having a birthday dinner tonight with a few friends over. But it's not my idea. Don't like it. Don't like being fussed over."

"How come? What's there about being fussed over that you don't like?"

"I feel uncomfortable with any kind of compliment. I kind of undo it with this inner voice saying, 'They don't really know me' or 'If they only knew.'"

"If they really knew you," I asked, "then they would see . . . what?"

"I don't even know myself. And it's not just receiving compliments that's awkward, but it's also giving them. Don't understand it and don't know how to put it except to say there's just another whole dark level there underneath. I can't access it."

"Are you aware, Will, of anything ever erupting from that level?"

"Yes, there is something. Death. Whenever I read a book about death, especially the death of a child, I choke up."

"Anything ever emerge from the dark level here with me?"

"I don't think so. Why? Are you thinking of something?"

"I'm thinking of a time in our first or second session when suddenly a strong emotion erupted and tears came to your eyes. You commented then that it was a rare thing for you to shed a tear. Can't quite remember the context. Do you?"

"I'm a total blank on it. In fact, I don't remember the incident at all."

"I believe it had something to do with your father. Here, let me check." I walked over to my computer, did a word search on "tears" in his file, and after a minute sat back down. "It *was* about your father. You were saying, sorrowfully, that you regretted never really talking personally to him, and suddenly you teared up."

"Oh yes, I remember and . . . oh, my God, I just remembered that I had a dream about him last night! I had no recollection of this dream before this very moment! If you had asked at the beginning of the hour whether I dreamed last night, I'd have said no. Well, in the dream I was talking to my father and my uncle. My father died about twelve years ago and my uncle a couple of years earlier. While the three of us were having a pleasant conversation about something, I could hear myself saying, 'They're dead, they're dead, but don't worry, this all makes sense, this is normal in a dream.'"

"Seems like the background voice-over is serving to keep the dream light, to keep you asleep. Do you often dream of your father?"

"Never before. Not that I remember."

"We're almost out of time, Will, but let me ask you something we talked about earlier—about giving and receiving compliments. Does that ever come into play here in this room? Between you and me? Earlier, when you described the pro bono case, I commented on your compassion. You didn't respond to me. I wonder how you felt about my saying something positive to you. And will you have a difficult time ever saying positive things to me?" (I rarely let an hour go by without making a here-and-now inquiry like this.)

"I'm not sure. I'll have to think about that," he said as he prepared to rise.

I added, "One last thing, Will. Tell me, what other feelings arose about our session and about me today?"

"A good session," he responded. "I was impressed you remembered the tears in my eyes from that earlier

session. But I've got to admit I started to feel real uncomfortable at the very end when you asked about my
feelings about your complimenting me or vice versa."

"Well, I'm convinced that such discomfort will be
a good guide to the most promising directions in our
work."

Note that in this therapy hour with Will, the
topic of death arose unexpectedly and spontaneously
when I inquired about his "dark level." It's rare for me
to get up and walk to my computer to consult my
notes midsession, but he was so cerebral that I wanted
to pursue the one display of emotion he had shown in
our sessions.

Consider all the existential issues I could have
turned to. First there was the occasion of his fiftieth
birthday. Such major birthdays usually have many internal ramifications. Then, when I inquired about his
hidden layer, he responded, to my surprise and with no
cueing from me, that he chokes up whenever he reads
about death, especially a child's death. And then the
sudden recall, again entirely unexpected, of the dream
in which he is talking to his dead father and uncle.

When I focused on his dream in following sessions, Will became aware of his hidden fear and sadness
about death—his father's death, the death of small children, and, behind those, his own death. We concluded
that he removed himself from feelings about death
because he felt the need to keep them from overtaking
him. Again and again he broke down in sessions, and I

helped him speak openly of his dark area and his here-tofore unspeakable fears.

DREAMS AS AWAKENING EXPERIENCES

If we listen to messages conveyed by powerful dreams we may be awakened. Consider this unforgettable dream told me by a young widow, mired in grief. It is a lucid example of how loss of a loved one can confront the bereaved with his or her own mortality:

I am in the screened porch of a flimsy summer cottage and see a large, menacing beast with an enormous mouth waiting a few feet from the front door. I am terrified. I worry something will happen to my daughter. I decide to try to satisfy the beast with a sacrifice and toss a red plaid stuffed animal out the door. The beast devours the bait but stays there. Its eyes burn. They are fixated on me. I am the prey.

This young widow clearly understood her dream. She thought at first that death (the menacing beast), which had already taken her husband, had now come for her daughter. But almost immediately she realized that she herself was imperiled. She was next in line, and the beast had come for her. She attempted to placate and distract the beast with a sacrifice, a red plaid stuffed animal. She knew, without my needing to ask, the meaning of that symbol: her husband had died wearing red plaid pajamas. But the beast was implacable: she was its prey. The compelling clarity of this dream ushered in a major shift in our therapy: she shifted away from her catastrophic loss toward a greater consideration of her own finiteness and how she should live.

The awakening experience is far from being a curious and rare concept; it is instead the bread and butter of clinical work. Consequently I spend much time teaching therapists how to identify and harness awakening experiences for therapeutic use—as in Mark's story, where a dream opened a door that led to their awakening.

A Grief Dream as an Awakening Experience: Mark

Mark, a forty-year-old psychotherapist, came to me for therapy because of chronic anxiety and intermittent panic attacks about dying. I saw how restless and agitated he was in our first session. He was painfully preoccupied with the death six years earlier of his older sister, Janet, who had functioned as a surrogate mother during his youth after his birth mother developed bone cancer when he was five and died ten years later after many recurrences and much disfiguring surgery.

During her early twenties, Janet became a chronic alcoholic and eventually died of liver failure. Despite his brotherly devotion to her—he had made scores of trips across the country to lend assistance during her illnesses—he could not shake the belief that he had not done enough, that he was guilty and in some way responsible for her death. His guilt was tenacious, and I encountered much difficulty in our therapy work in moving him past it.

As I have said, a potential awakening experience lies in almost every course of grief and often makes its first appearance in a dream. In one of Mark's frequent nightmares, he described an image of blood gushing from his sister's hand—an image that recalled an early memory. When he was about five, his sister was at a neighbor's home and put her thumb into an electric fan. He recalled seeing her running down the street screaming. There was blood, so much crimson blood, and so much terror, both hers and his.

He recalled the thought he had (or must have had) as a child: if his protector, Janet—so big, so capable, so strong—was in truth fragile and so easily brought down, then he *really* had something to fear. How can she possibly protect him if she cannot protect herself? That being so, lurking in his unconscious there must have been the equation, *If my sister has to die, then so must I.*

As we discussed his fears of death more openly, he became more agitated. In my office he often paced about as we spoke. In his life he was always on the move, scheduling one trip after another, visiting new places on every possible occasion. More than once the thought crossed his mind that sinking permanent roots anywhere would make him a sitting duck for the Grim Reaper: he felt that his life, indeed all of life, was merely a holding pattern awaiting death.

Gradually, after a year of hard work in therapy, he had the following illuminating dream, which ushered in his letting go of his guilt about his sister's death:

My aged uncle and aunt are going to visit Janet, who is seven squares away. [At this point Mark asked for paper and sketched a seven-by-seven grid of the dream's geography.] They are going to cross the river to get to her. I knew I would have to visit her too, but I had things to do and decided to stay home for now. As they prepare to leave, I think of a small gift for them to take to Janet. Then as they are driving away, I remembered I had forgotten a card to accompany the gift and run after them. I recall what the card looked like—rather formal and distant—and signed "to Janet, from your brother." In some curious way, I can see Janet standing on the grid on the other side of the river, possibly waving. But I felt little emotion.

The imagery in this dream is exceptionally transparent. The aged relatives die (that is, cross the river) and go to visit Janet seven squares away. (At this point in Mark's therapy, Janet had been dead seven years.) Mark decided to stay behind even though he knew he would have to cross the river later. He had things to do and knew that to stay in life, he would have to let go of his sister (as indicated by the formal card accompanying the gift and his lack of distress on seeing her waving to him across the grid).

The dream heralded a change: Mark's obsession with the past faded and he gradually learned to live life more richly in the present.

Dreams opened a door for many of my other patients as well, including Ray, a retiring surgeon, and Kevan, who had reached the point when our work together was finished and he was leaving therapy.

The Retiring Surgeon: Ray

Ray, a sixty-eight-year-old surgeon, sought therapy because of persistent anxiety about his impending retirement. In his second therapy session, he reported this short dream fragment:

I go to a reunion of my school class, perhaps the sixth grade. I enter the building and see the class picture posted at the entrance. I looked at it carefully for a long time and saw all the faces of my classmates, but I was missing. I could not find myself.

"What was the feeling in the dream?" I asked. (Always my first question, as it's particularly useful to find the emotions associated with the entire dream or parts of it.)

"Hard to say," he responded. "The dream was heavy or sober—definitely not cheerful."

"Tell me about your associations to the dream. Do you still see the dream in your mind's eye?" (The fresher the dream, the more likely that the patient's associations will yield useful information.)

He nodded. "Well, the picture is the main thing. I see it clearly—I can't make out many of the faces, but I know somehow that I'm not there. I can't find myself."

"And what do you make of that?"

"Can't be sure—but two possibilities. First there's my feeling about never being a part of that class—or any class. I was never popular. Always the outsider. Except in the OR [operating room]." He paused.

"And the second possibility?" I prompted.

"Well, the obvious one," his voice dropped. "The class is there in the photo, but I'm missing—probably suggests or predicts my death?"

Thus, through the dream, much rich material emerged and offered several possible directions. For example, I could have explored Ray's sense of not belonging, his unpopularity, his lack of friends, his not feeling at home anywhere but the operating room. Or I could have concentrated on his phrase "I can't find myself" and focused on his sense of being out of touch with his core. The dream set the agenda for the year's course of therapy during which we worked on these issues.

But, most of all, my attention was riveted to one thing: his absence from his class photo. His comment about his death seemed the most relevant issue; after all, he was a sixty-eight-year-old man whose impending retirement brought him to therapy. Anyone considering retirement has lurking concerns about death, and not infrequently these concerns make their appearance by way of a dream.

THE END OF THERAPY AS AN AWAKENING EXPERIENCE

A Dream About the End of Therapy: Kevan

In his final session, Kevan, a forty-year-old engineer, whose periodic death panics had almost entirely disappeared during fourteen months of therapy, had this dream:

I am being chased in a long building. Don't know by whom. I am frightened and run down the stairs into a kind of basement region. At one spot I see sand falling down from the ceiling in a trickle as though it is an hourglass. It is dark; I go further and can find no way out and then suddenly at the end of corridor in the basement I see huge warehouse doors slightly open. Even though I feel scared, I walk through the doors.

The feelings in this dark dream? "Fear and heaviness," Kevan responded. I asked him for associations, but few came; the dream seemed to him a blank. From my existential perspective, I felt that his finishing therapy and saying farewell to me might well have evoked in him thoughts of other losses and of death. Two images in the dream particularly caught my attention: the sand falling as though in an hourglass and the warehouse doors. Rather than express my ideas about these, however, I prodded Kevan to associate to these images.

"What does the hourglass bring to mind?"

"Thoughts about time. Time running out. Life half over."

"And the warehouse?"

"Bodies warehoused. A morgue."

"It's our last session, Kevan. Our time here is running out."

"Yeah, I was just thinking that, too."

"And the morgue and warehoused bodies: you haven't spoken about death for several weeks. Yet that's why you came to see me originally. Looks like our ending therapy is bringing up old issues for you."

"I think so—I'm now questioning whether we're really ready to stop."

Experienced therapists know not to take such questioning so seriously as to extend therapy. Patients who have had a meaningful course of therapy usually approach termination with much ambivalence and often experience a recrudescence of their original symptoms. Someone once referred to psychotherapy as cyclotherapy: one goes over the same issues again and again, each time securing the personal change more tightly. I suggested to Kevan that we terminate our work as planned but have a follow-up meeting in two months. At that meeting Kevan was doing well and was well into the process of transferring what he had gained from therapy into his outside life.

Awakening experiences thus range from the deathbed experience of Ivan Ilych to the near-death experiences of many cancer patients to more subtle confrontations in everyday life (such as birthdays, grief, reunions, dreams, the empty nest) where the individual is primed to examine existential issues. Awakening consciousness can often be facilitated by the help of another—a friend or therapist—with a greater sensibility to these issues (obtained, it is my hope, from these pages).

Keep in mind the point of these incursions: *that a confrontation with death arouses anxiety but also has the potential of vastly enriching life.* Awakening experiences may be powerful but ephemeral. The following chapters will discuss how we can make the experience more enduring.

Chapter 4

THE POWER
OF IDEAS

———

I deas have power. The insights of many great
thinkers and writers through the centuries help us
quell roiling thoughts about death and discover meaningful paths through life. In this chapter, I discuss those
ideas that have proved most useful in my therapy with
patients haunted by death anxiety.

EPICURUS AND HIS AGELESS WISDOM

———

Epicurus believed that the proper mission of philosophy
is to relieve human misery. And the root cause of human misery? Epicurus had no doubt about the answer
to that question: *it is our omnipresent fear of death.*

The frightening thought of inevitable death, Epicurus insisted, interferes with our enjoyment of life and leaves no pleasure undisturbed. Because no activity can satisfy our craving for eternal life, all activities are intrinsically unrewarding. He wrote that many individuals develop a hatred of life—even, ironically, to the point of suicide; others engage in frenetic and aimless activity that has no point other than the avoidance of the pain inherent in the human condition.

Epicurus addressed the unending and unsatisfying search for novel activities by urging that we store and recall deeply etched memories of pleasant experiences. If we can learn to draw on such memories again and again, he suggested, we will have no need for endless hedonistic pursuit.

Legend has it that he followed his own advice, and on his deathbed (of complications following kidney stones) Epicurus retained equanimity despite searing pain by recalling pleasurable conversations with his circle of friends and students.

It is part of Epicurus's genius to have anticipated the contemporary view of the unconscious: he emphasized that death concerns are not conscious to most individuals but must be inferred by disguised manifestations: for example, excessive religiosity, an all-consuming accumulation of wealth, and blind grasping for power and honors, all of which offer a counterfeit version of immortality.

How did Epicurus attempt to alleviate death anxiety? He formulated a series of well-constructed arguments, which his students memorized like a catechism. Many of these arguments have been debated over the past twenty-three hundred years and are still germane to overcoming the fear of death. In this chapter, I will discuss three of his best-known arguments, which I've found valuable in my work with many patients and to me personally in relieving my own death anxiety.

1. The mortality of the soul
2. The ultimate nothingness of death
3. The argument of symmetry

The Mortality of the Soul

Epicurus taught that the soul is mortal and perishes with the body, a conclusion diametrically opposite to that of Socrates, who, shortly before his execution one hundred years earlier, had found comfort in his belief in the immortality of the soul and in the expectation that it would thereafter enjoy the eternal community of like-minded people sharing his search for wisdom. Much of Socrates' position—fully described in the Platonic dialogue the *Phaedo*—was adopted and preserved by the Neo-Platonists and ultimately was to exert considerable influence on the Christian structure of the afterlife.

Epicurus was vehement in his condemnation of contemporary religious leaders who, in an effort to increase their own power, increased the death anxiety of their followers by warning of the punishments that would be meted out after death to those who failed to heed particular rules and regulations. (In the centuries to follow, the religious iconography of medieval Christianity depicting the punishments of Hell—as in the fifteenth-century Last Judgment scenes painted by Hieronymus Bosch—added a gory visual dimension to death anxiety.)

If we are mortal and the soul does not survive, Epicurus insisted, then we have nothing to fear in an afterlife. We will have no consciousness, no regrets for the life that was lost, nor anything to fear from the gods. Epicurus did not deny the existence of gods (that argument would had been perilous, Socrates having been executed on the charge of heresy less than a century before), but he did claim that the gods were oblivious to human life and only useful to us as models of tranquility and bliss toward which we should aspire.

The Ultimate Nothingness of Death

In his second argument, Epicurus posits that death is nothing to us, because the soul is mortal and is dispersed at death. What is dispersed does not perceive, and anything not perceived is nothing to us. In other words: where I am, death is not; where death is, I am not. Therefore, Epicurus held, "why fear death when we can never perceive it?"

Epicurus's position is the ultimate counter to Woody Allen's quip, "I'm not afraid of death, I just don't want to be there when it happens." Epicurus is saying that indeed we won't be there, that we won't know when it happens because death and "I" can never coexist. Because we are dead, we don't know that we are dead, and, in that case, what is there to fear?

The Argument of Symmetry

Epicurus's third argument holds that our state of non-being after death is the same state we were in before our birth. Despite many philosophical disputes about this ancient argument, I believe that it still retains the power to provide comfort to the dying.

Of the many who have restated this argument over the centuries, none has done so more beautifully than Vladimir Nabokov, the great Russian novelist, in his autobiography, *Speak, Memory,* which begins with these lines: "The cradle rocks above an abyss, and common sense tells us that our existence is but a brief crack of light between two eternities of darkness. Although the two are identical twins, man, as a rule, views the prenatal abyss with more calm than the one he is heading for (at some forty-five hundred heartbeats an hour)."

I have personally found it comforting on many occasions to think that the two states of nonbeing—the time before our birth and the time after death—are identical and that we have so much fear about the second pool of darkness and so little concern about the first.

An e-mail from a reader contains relevant sentiments:

At this time I am more or less comfortable with the idea of oblivion. It seems the only logical conclusion. Ever since I was a small child I thought that after death one must logically return to the state before birth. Ideas of afterlife seemed incongruous and convoluted compared with the simplicity of that conclusion. I could not console myself with the idea of an afterlife because the idea of unending existence, whether pleasant or unpleasant, is far more terrifying to me than that of a finite existence.

Generally I introduce the ideas of Epicurus early in my work with patients suffering from death terror. They serve both to introduce a patient to the ideational work of therapy and convey my willingness to relate to him or her—namely, that I am willing to enter that person's inner chambers of fear and have some aids to ease our journey. Although some patients find Epicurus's ideas irrelevant and insubstantial, many find in them comfort and help—perhaps because they remind them of the universality of their concerns and that great souls like Epicurus grappled with the same issue.

RIPPLING

Of all the ideas that have emerged from my years of practice to counter a person's death anxiety and distress at the transience of life, I have found the idea of *rippling* singularly powerful.

Rippling refers to the fact that each of us creates—often without our conscious intent or knowledge—concentric circles of influence that may affect others for years, even for generations. That is, the effect we have on other people is in turn passed on to others, much as the ripples in a pond go on and on until they're no longer visible but continuing at a nano level. The idea that we can leave something of ourselves, even beyond our knowing, offers a potent answer to those who claim that meaninglessness inevitably flows from one's finiteness and transiency.

Rippling does not necessarily mean leaving behind your image or your name. Many of us learned the futility of that strategy long ago in our school curriculum when we read these lines from Shelley's poem about a huge shattered antique statue in a now barren land:

> *My name is Ozymandias, King of Kings*
> *Look on my Works, ye Mighty, and despair.*

Attempts to preserve personal identity are always futile. Transiency is forever. Rippling, as I use it, refers instead to leaving behind something from your life experience; some trait; some piece of wisdom, guidance, virtue, comfort that passes on to others, known or unknown. The story of Barbara is illustrative.

"Look for Her Among Her Friends": Barbara

Barbara, who had been plagued by death anxiety for many years, reported two events that markedly reduced her anxiety.

The first event occurred at a school reunion, when, for the first time in thirty years, she saw Allison, a close, slightly younger friend from early adolescence, who ran up to her, smothered her with embraces and kisses, and thanked her for the vast amount of guidance she had provided when they were teens together.

Barbara had long before intuited the general concept of rippling. As a schoolteacher, she had taken it for granted that she influenced her students in ways entirely divorced from their memory of her. But her encounter with her forgotten childhood friend made rippling far more real to her. She was pleased and a bit surprised to learn that so much of her advice and guidance persisted in the memory of a childhood friend, but she was truly shocked the following day when she met Allison's thirteen-year-old daughter, who was visibly thrilled to meet her mother's legendary friend.

While reflecting on the plane home about the re-union, Barbara had an epiphany that permitted her a new perspective on death. Perhaps death was not quite the annihilation she had thought. Perhaps it was not so essential that her person *or even memories of her person* survived. Perhaps the important thing was that her ripples persist, ripples of some act or idea that would help others attain joy and virtue in life, ripples that would fill her with pride and act to counter the immorality, horror, and violence monopolizing the mass media and the outside world.

These thoughts were reinforced by the second event, two months later, when her mother died and she delivered a short talk for the funeral service. One of her mother's favorite phrases came to mind: *Look for her among her friends.*

This phrase had power: she knew that her mother's caring, gentleness, and love of life lived inside her, her only child. As she delivered the talk and scanned the funeral assemblage, she could physically feel aspects of her mother that had rippled into her friends, who in turn would pass the ripples on to their children and children's children.

Since childhood, nothing had terrified Barbara more than the thought of nothingness. The Epicurean arguments I offered were ineffective. She was, for example, not relieved when I pointed out that she would never experience the horror of nothingness because her awareness would not exist after death. But the idea of rippling—of continued existence through the acts of caring and help and love she passed on to others—greatly attenuated her fear.

"Look for her among her friends"—what comfort, what a powerful framework of life-meaning, resided in that idea. As I discuss further in Chapter Five, I believe that the secular message of Everyman, the medieval religious drama, is that Good Deeds accompany one to death and will ripple on to succeeding generations.

Barbara returned to the cemetery a year later for the unveiling of her mother's tombstone and experienced a variant of rippling. Rather than being depressed by the sight of her mother's and father's graves situated amidst those of a large number of relatives, she experienced an extraordinary sense of relief and lightening of her spirits. Why? She found it hard to put into words: the closest she could come to it was, "If they can do it, then so can I." Even in death her forbears passed something on to her.

Other Examples of Rippling

Examples of rippling are legion and well known. Who has not experienced a glow upon learning that one has been, directly or indirectly, important to another? In Chapter Six I discuss how my own mentors rippled into me and, through these pages, to you. Indeed, my desire to be of value to others is largely what keeps me pecking away at my keyboard long past the standard time for retirement.

In *The Gift of Therapy,* I describe an incident where a patient who had lost her hair because of radiotherapy had felt extreme discomfort about her appearance and was fearful that someone would see her without her wig. When she took a risk by removing her wig in my office, I responded by gently running my fingers through her few remaining wisps of hair. Years later, I saw her again for a brief course of therapy, and she told me that she had recently reread the passage about her in my book and felt joy that I had recorded this piece of her and passed it on to other therapists and patients. It gave her pleasure, she said, to learn that her experience might in some way benefit others even those unknown to her.

Rippling is cousin to many strategies that share the heart-wrenching longing to project oneself into the future. Most apparent is the desire to project oneself biologically through children transmitting our genes, or through organ donation, in which our heart beats for another and our corneas permit vision. About twenty years ago, I had corneal replacements in each eye, and though I do not know the identity of the dead donor, I often experience a wave of gratitude to that unknown person.

Other rippling effects include

A rise to prominence through political, artistic,
   or financial achievement

Leaving one's name on buildings, institutes,
   foundations, and scholarships

Making a contribution to basic science, on which
   other scientists will build

Rejoining nature through one's scattered
   molecules, which may serve as building blocks
   for future life

Perhaps I've focused particularly on rippling because my vantage point as a therapist gives me an unusually privileged view of the silent, gentle, intangible transmission that occurs from one individual to another.

The Japanese director Akira Kurosawa powerfully portrays the process of rippling in his 1952 film masterpiece, *Ikiru,* which continues to be shown worldwide. This is the story of Watanabe, a servile Japanese bureaucrat who learns he has stomach cancer and only a few months to live. The cancer serves as an awakening experience for this man, who had previously lived such a narrow life that his employees had nicknamed him "the mummy."

After learning his diagnosis, he skips work for the first time in thirty years, takes a large sum of money from his bank account, and tries to spend his way back into life in vibrant Japanese night clubs. At the end of his futile spending spree, he chances on an ex-employee who left her job at his agency because it was too deadening. She wanted to live! Fascinated by her vitality and energy, he pursues her and begs her to teach him how to live. She can inform him only that she hated her old job because it was meaningless bureaucracy. In her new job making dolls in a toy factory, she is inspired by the thought of bringing happiness to many children. When he tells her of his cancer and his nearness to death, she is filled with dread and rushes away, flinging him only a single, over-the-shoulder message: "Make something."

Watanabe returns, transformed, to his job, refuses to be bound by bureaucratic ritual, breaks all the rules, and dedicates his remaining life to the creation of a neighborhood park that children will enjoy for generations. In the last scene Watanabe, near death, is sitting on a swing in the park. Despite the flurries of snow, he is serene, and approaches death with a new-found equanimity.

The phenomenon of rippling, of creating something that will be passed on and that will enlarge the life of others, transforms his terror into deep satisfaction. The film emphasizes, too, that it is the park, not the transmission of his identity, that is paramount. In fact, at his wake, the drunken municipal bureaucrats enter into a lengthy ironic discussion of whether Watanabe should be given any credit whatsoever for the creation of the park.

Rippling and Transiency

Many individuals report that they rarely think of their own death but are obsessed with the idea, and the terror, of transiency. Every pleasant moment is corroded by the background thought that everything now experienced is evanescent and will end shortly. An enjoyable walk with a friend is undermined by the thought that everything is slated to vanish—the friend will die, this forest will be transformed by creeping urban development. What's the point in anything if everything will turn to dust?

Freud states the argument (and the counterargument) beautifully in an incidental short essay, "On Transience," that recounts a summer walk he took with two companions, a poet and an analytic colleague. The poet lamented that all beauty is destined to fade into nothingness and that all he loved was shorn of its value by its ultimate disappearance. Freud disputed the poet's gloomy conclusion and vigorously denied that transiency negates value or meaning.

"On the contrary," he exclaimed. "An increase! Limitation in the possibility of an enjoyment raises the value of the enjoyment." Then he offered a powerful counterargument to the idea that meaninglessness is inherent in transiency:

> It was incomprehensible, I declared, that the thought of the transience of beauty should interfere with our

joy in it. As regards the beauty of Nature, each time it
is destroyed by winter it comes again next year, so that
in relation to the length of our lives it can in fact be
regarded as eternal. The beauty of the human form
and face vanish for ever in the course of our own lives,
but their evanescence only lends them a fresh charm.
A flower that blossoms only for a single night does not
seem to us in that account less lovely. Nor can I understand any better why the beauty and perfection of a
work of art or of an intellectual achievement should
lose its worth because of its temporal limitation. A time
may indeed come when the pictures and statues which
we admire today will crumble to dust, or a race of men
may follow us who no longer understand the works
of our poets and thinkers, or a geological epoch may
even arrive when all animate life upon the earth ceases;
but since the value of all this beauty and perfection is
determined only by its significance for our own emotional lives, it has no need to survive us and is therefore
independent of absolute duration.

Thus Freud attempts to soften death's terror by
separating human esthetics and values from death's
grasp and positing that transiency has no claim on what
is vitally significant for an individual's emotional life.

Many traditions try to gather power over transiency by stressing the importance of living in the moment and focusing on immediate experience. Buddhist
practice, for example, includes a series of meditations

on *anicca* (impermanence) in which one focuses on the desiccation and disappearance of leaves from a tree and then on the future impermanence of the tree itself and, indeed, of one's own body. One might think of this practice as a "deconditioning," or a type of exposure therapy whereby one habituates to the fear by pointedly immersing oneself in it. Perhaps reading this book will have a similar effect on some readers.

Rippling tempers the pain of transiency by reminding us that something of each us persists even though it may be unknown or imperceptible to us.

MIGHTY THOUGHTS TO HELP OVERCOME DEATH ANXIETY

A few pithy lines or an aphorism by a philosopher or other thinker can often help us reflect usefully on our own death anxiety and life fulfillment. Whether through the ingenuity of the phrasing, the rhetoric, or the ring of its lines, or through being tightly coiled, crammed with kinetic energy—such mighty thoughts can jolt a solitary reader or a patient out of a familiar, but static, mode of being. Perhaps, as I've suggested, it's comforting to know that giants of thought have themselves struggled with, and triumphed over, similar grievous concerns. Or perhaps such memorable words demonstrate that despair can be transformed into art.

Nietzsche, the greatest aphorist of all, provides the most pointed description of the power of mighty thoughts: "A good aphorism is too hard for the tooth of time and is not consumed by all millennia, although it serves every time for nourishment: thus it is the great paradox of literature, the intransitory amid the changing, the food that always remains esteemed, like salt, and never loses its savor."

Some of these aphorisms pertain explicitly to death anxiety; others encourage us to look deeper and resist being consumed by trivial concerns.

"Everything Fades: Alternatives Exclude"

In John Gardner's wonderful novel *Grendel,* the tormented monster in the Beowulf legend seeks out a wise man to learn the answer to life's mystery. The wise man tells him, "The ultimate evil is that Time is perpetually perishing, and being actual involves elimination." He summed up his life meditations with four inspired words, two terse, profound propositions: "Everything fades: alternatives exclude."

As I've already had much to say about "everything fades," let me turn to the implications of the second proposition. "Alternatives exclude" is the underlying reason many people are driven to distraction by the necessity to make a decision. For every yes there must be a no, and every positive choice means you have to relinquish others. Many of us shrink from fully apprehending the limits, diminishment, and loss that are riveted to existence.

For example, relinquishment was an enormous problem for Les, a thirty-seven-year-old physician, who agonized for years over which of several women he wanted to marry. When he finally married, he moved into his wife's home a hundred miles away and opened a second office in his new community. Nonetheless, for several years he kept his old office open one-and-a-half days a week and spent a night each week seeing old girlfriends.

In therapy we focused on his resistance to saying no to other alternatives. As I pressed him on what it would mean to say no—that is, close his office and end his affairs—he gradually became aware of his grandiose self-image. He had been the family's multitalented golden boy—a musician, athlete, national honors winner in science. He knew he could have succeeded at any profession he chose, and he viewed himself as someone exempt from the limitations of others, someone who should not have to give up anything. "Alternatives exclude" might apply to others, but not to him. His personal myth was that life was an eternal spiral upward, into a bigger and better future, and he resisted anything that threatened that myth.

At first it seemed that Les's therapy needed to focus on issues of lust, fidelity, and indecisiveness, but ultimately it required an exploration of deeper, existential issues: his belief that he was both destined to continue growing larger and brighter and, at the same time, remain exempt from the limitations imposed on other mortal creatures, even death. Les (like Pat in Chapter Three) was sharply threatened by anything that hinted at relinquishment: he was attempting to evade the rule of "alternatives exclude," and the clarification of this attempt sharpened our focus and accelerated our future work in therapy. Once he could accept relinquishment and turn his attention away from frantically holding on to everything he had ever had, we were able to work on his experiencing life and particularly his relationships with his wife and children in the immediate present.

The belief that life is a perpetual upward spiral often arises in psychotherapy. I once treated a fifty-year-old woman whose seventy-year-old husband, an eminent scientist, developed dementia from a stroke. She was particularly unsettled by the sight of her ailing husband doing nothing but sit in front of the TV all day. Try as hard as she could, she simply could not restrain herself from haranguing him to do something, anything, to improve his mind: read a book, play chess, work on his Spanish, do crossword puzzles. Her husband's dementia had shattered her vision of life as always ascending toward greater learning, more discoveries and acclaim; and the alternative was hard to bear—that each of us is finite and destined to traverse the passage from infancy and childhood through maturity to ultimate decline.

"When We Are Tired, We Are Attacked by Ideas We Conquered Long Ago"

Nietzsche's phrase played a role in my work with Kate, a divorced physician, whom I had seen three previous times. She consulted me this time, at the age of sixty-eight, with pervasive anxiety about impending retirement, aging, and fear of death.

Once, during the course of therapy, she woke at four in the morning and, slipping in the bathroom, suffered a deep gash in her scalp. Though she bled heavily, she did not call her neighbors or her children or the emergency room. Her hair had thinned so much that she had started wearing a hairpiece and could not face the ordeal of appearing without it, an old bald woman, before her colleagues at the hospital.

So she grabbed a towel, cold pack, and a quart of coffee ice cream and lay in bed, applying pressure to her head with the towel and cold pack, eating the ice cream, weeping for her mother (now twenty-two years dead), and feeling entirely abandoned. When dawn arrived, she called her son, who took her to the private office of a colleague. He sutured her wound and instructed her not to wear her wig for at least a week.

When I saw Kate three days later, her head was swathed in a shawl, and she was awash with shame about her wig, her divorce, her single status in a culture of couples. Shame, too, about her coarse, psychotic mother (who always fed her coffee ice cream when she was unhappy), about the poverty endured during her entire childhood, and about the irresponsible father who had abandoned the family when she was a child. She felt defeated. She felt she had made no progress after two years of therapy, nor in her earlier courses of therapy.

Not wishing to be seen without her wig, she spent the entire week indoors (aside from our one session) doing a massive housecleaning. While cleaning out closets, she discovered notes she had made of our past therapy sessions and was shocked to discover that we had discussed the exact same issues twenty years earlier. We had not only worked to alleviate shame but had labored long and hard to liberate her from her disturbed, intrusive mother, then still alive.

Notes in hand, her head covered with a stylish turban, she came in for her next hour highly discouraged about her lack of progress.

"I came to see you because of issues about aging and fears of dying, and here I am again, in the same place, after all these years, full of shame, yearning for my crazy mother and soothing myself with her coffee ice cream."

"Kate, I know how you must feel to be bringing up such old material. Let me tell you something that might help, something Nietzsche said a century ago: 'When we are tired, we are attacked by ideas we conquered long ago.'"

Kate, who ordinarily never allowed a moment of silence and usually spoke in rapid-fire, cogent sentences and paragraphs, was suddenly quiet.

I repeated Nietzsche's phrase. She nodded slowly, and by the following session we were back at work on her concerns about her aging and her fears for the future.

The aphorism contained nothing new: I had already reassured her that she had simply undergone a regression as a response to her trauma. Yet the elegant phrasing and the reminder that her experience was shared even by a great spirit like Nietzsche helped her grasp that her toxic state of mind was only temporary. It helped her appreciate, in her bones, that she had once conquered her inner demons and would do so once again. Good ideas, even ideas of power, are rarely sufficient in a single shot: repeated doses are necessary.

Living the Identical Life, Over and Over Again, for All Eternity

In *Thus Spake Zarathustra,* Nietzsche portrayed an aged prophet, ripe with wisdom, who decides to come down from the mountaintop and share with people what he has learned.

Of all the ideas he preaches, there is one he considers his "mightiest thought"—the idea of eternal recurrence. Zarathustra poses a challenge: what if you were to live the identical life again and again throughout eternity—how would that change you? The following chilling words are his first description of the "eternal return" thought experiment. I have often read them aloud to patients. Try reading them aloud to yourself.

> What if some day or night, a demon were to steal
> after you into your loneliest loneliness and say to you:
> "This life as you now live it and have lived it, you will
> have to live once more and innumerable times more;
> and there will be nothing new in it, but every pain
> and every joy and every thought and sigh and every-
> thing unutterably small or great in your life will
> have to return to you, all in the same succession
> and sequence—even this spider and this moonlight
> between the trees, and even this moment and I myself.
> The eternal hourglass of existence is turned upside
> down again and again, and you with it, speck of dust!"
> Would you not throw yourself down and gnash your
> teeth and curse the demon who spoke thus? Or have
> you once experienced a tremendous moment when
> you would have answered him: "You are a god and
> never have I heard anything more divine." If this
> thought gained possession of you, it would change
> you as you are, or perhaps crush you.

The idea of living your identical life again and again for all eternity can be jarring, a sort of *petite* existential shock therapy. It often serves as a sobering thought experiment, leading you to consider seriously how you are really living. Like the Ghost of Christmas Yet to Come, it increases your awareness that this life, your *only* life, should be lived well and fully, accumulating as few regrets as possible. Nietzsche thus serves as a guide leading us away from the preoccupation with trivial concerns to the goal of living vitally.

No positive change can occur in your life as long as you cling to the thought that the reason for your not living well lies outside yourself. As long as you place responsibility entirely on others who treat you unfairly—a loutish husband, a demanding and unsupportive boss, bad genes, irresistible compulsions—then your situation will remain at an impasse. *You and you alone* are responsible for the crucial aspects of your life situation, and only you have the power to change it. And even if you face overwhelming external restraints, you still have the freedom and the choice of adopting various attitudes toward those restraints.

One of Nietzsche's favorite phrases is *amor fati* (love your fate): in other words, *create the fate that you can love.*

At first Nietzsche advanced the idea of eternal return as a serious proposal. If time were infinite, he reasoned, and matter were finite, then all various arrangements of matter would have to recur randomly again and again, much like the hypothetical army of monkey typists who by random chance over the course of a billion years produce Shakespeare's *Hamlet*. The mathematics falters here and has been heavily criticized by logicians. Years ago when I visited Pforta, the school where Nietzsche had been educated from the age of fourteen until twenty, I was permitted to browse through his report cards, which showed that he received very high grades in Greek and Latin and classical studies (though he was *not,* the aged archivist who acted as my guide was careful to point out, the very best classical scholar in his class) but particularly poor grades in mathematics. Ultimately Nietzsche, perhaps aware that such speculation was not his strong suit, focused more exclusively on eternal return as a thought experiment.

If you engage in this experiment and find the thought painful or even unbearable, there is one obvious explanation: you do not believe you've lived your life well. I would proceed by posing such questions as, How have you not lived well? What regrets do you have about your life?

My purpose is not to drown anyone in a sea of regret for the past but, ultimately, to turn his or her gaze toward the future and this potentially life-changing question: *What can you do now in your life so that one year or five years from now, you won't look back and have similar dismay about the new regrets you've accumulated? In other words, can you find a way to live without continuing to accumulate regrets?*

Nietzsche's thought experiment provides a powerful tool for the clinician to help those whose death anxiety stems from the sense of having failed to having lived life fully. Dorothy provides us with a clinical illustration.

THE 10 PERCENT PORTION: DOROTHY Dorothy, a forty-year-old bookkeeper, felt a pervasive sense of being trapped in life. She was awash in regrets about myriad actions, such as her unwillingness to forgive her husband for an affair, which had led to her decision to end her marriage; for her failure to reconcile with her father before he died; for allowing herself to be caught in an unrewarding job in an unpleasant geographical location.

One day she saw an advertisement for a job in Portland, Oregon, which she considered a more desirable place to live, and, for a short while, seriously considered relocating. Her excitement was quickly quelled, however, by a tidal wave of discouraging negative thoughts: she was too old to move, her children would hate to leave their friends, she knew no one in Portland, the pay was lower, she could not be certain she'd like her new work colleagues.

"So I had hope for a while," she said, "but you see I'm as trapped as ever."

"Seems to me," I responded, "that you're both trapped and trapper. I understand how these circumstances may prevent you from changing your life, but I wonder whether they account for everything. Let's say that all these real-life, out-of-your control reasons—your children, your age, money, your unpleasant coworkers—account for, say, ninety percent of your inertia; still I wonder if there's not some portion that belongs to you—even if it's only ten percent?"

She nodded.

"Well, it's *that* ten percent that we want to examine here in our therapy because *that's* the part, the only part, you can change." At this point, I described Nietzsche's thought experiment and read aloud the passage about eternal return. I then asked Dorothy to project herself into the future in accord with it. I wound up with this suggestion: "Let's pretend a year has gone by, and we are meeting again in this office. Okay?"

Dorothy nodded, "Okay, but I think I see where this is going."

"Even so, let's try it out. It's a year from now." I begin the role play: "So, Dorothy, let's look back over this past year. Tell me, what new regrets do you have? Or, in the language of Nietzsche's thought experiment, would you be willing to live this past year again and again for all eternity?"

"Nope, no way I want to live fixed in that trap forever—three kids, little money, awful job, still stuck."

"Now let's look at your responsibility, your ten percent, for the way things have gone this past year. What regrets do you have about your actions the last twelve months? What might you have done differently?"

"Well, the jail door was open, just a crack, once—that job possibility in Portland."

"And if you had the year to live over . . ."

"Yeah, yeah, I get the point. I'm probably going to be spending this next year regretting not even trying for that position in Portland."

"Right, that's exactly what I mean by your being both the prisoner and the jailer."

Dorothy did apply for the position, was interviewed, visited the community, was offered the position, but ultimately turned it down after checking out the schools, weather, real estate prices, and cost of living. The process, however, opened her eyes (and her jail door). She felt differently about herself simply because she had seriously considered a move; four months later, she applied for, obtained, and accepted a better position closer to home.

———

Nietzsche claimed two "granite" sentences that were hard enough to withstand the erosion of time: "Become who you are" and "That which does not kill me makes me stronger." And so they have, both having entered the general vernacular of therapy. We'll examine each in turn.

"Become Who You Are"

The concept of the first granite sentence—"Become who you are"—was familiar to Aristotle and passed on through Spinoza, Leibnitz, Goethe, Nietzsche, Ibsen, Karen Horney, Abraham Maslow, and the 1960s human potential movement, down to our contemporary idea of self-realization.

The concept of becoming "who you are" is closely connected to other Nietzsche pronouncements, "Consummate your life" and "Die at the right time." In all these variants Nietzsche exhorted us to avoid unlived life. He was saying, fulfill yourself, realize your potential, live boldly and fully. *Then, and only then,* die without regret.

For example, Jennie, a thirty-one-year-old legal secretary, consulted me because of severe death anxiety. After the fourth session, she dreamed:

I'm in Washington, where I was born, and I'm walking in the city with my grandmother, now dead. Then we came to a beautiful neighborhood with homes that were mansions. The mansion we went to was enormous and all white. An old friend from high school lived there with her family. I was happy to see her, and she showed me around her home. I was amazed—it was beautiful and full of rooms. It had thirty-one rooms, and they are all furnished! I then said to her, "My house has five rooms, and only two are furnished." I woke up very anxious, and furious with my husband.

Her intuitions about the dream were that the thirty-one rooms represented her thirty-one years and all the different areas of herself that she needed to explore. The fact that her own house had only five rooms and only two that were furnished reinforced the idea that she was not living her life correctly. The presence of her grandmother, who had died three months earlier, cloaked the dream in dread.

Her dream opened up our work dramatically. I asked about her anger at her husband, and, with much embarrassment, she revealed that he had often beaten her. She knew that she had to do something about her life, but she was terrified of leaving her marriage: she had little experience with men and felt certain she could never find another man. Her self-esteem was so low that for several years, she put up with his abuse rather than lay her marriage on the line and confront her husband with a demand for major changes. She didn't return home after that session, but instead went directly to her parents and stayed with them for several weeks. She gave her husband an ultimatum that he had to enter couples therapy. He complied, and a year of couples therapy and individual therapy resulted in a major improvement in her marriage.

"That Which Does Not Kill Me Makes Me Stronger"

Nietzsche's second granite sentence has been used, and overused, by many contemporary writers. It was, for example, one of Hemingway's favorite themes. (In *A Farewell to Arms* he added, "we become stronger in the broken places.") Still, the concept is a powerful reminder that adverse experience can leave one stronger and more able to adapt to adversity. This aphorism is closely related to Nietzsche's idea that a tree, by weathering storms and sinking its roots deep into the earth, grows stronger and taller.

Another variant on this theme was offered by one of my patients, an effective and resourceful woman, who was CEO of a major industrial company. As a child she had suffered vicious and continual verbal abuse from her father. In one session she described a daydream, a fanciful idea of futuristic therapy.

"In my daydream I was seeing a therapist who possessed the technology of total memory erasure. Maybe I got the idea from that Jim Carrey movie *Eternal Sunshine of the Spotless Mind.* I imagined that one day the therapist asked me if I wished her to do a total erasure of all memory of my father's existence. All I would know was that there had been no father in the home. That sounded great at first. But then as I pondered it further, I realized it was a tough call."

"Why a tough call?"

"Well, at first, it seems a no-brainer: my father was a monster and terrified me and my sibs throughout childhood. But, in the end, I decided to leave my memory alone and have none of it erased. Despite the wretched abuse I suffered, I have succeeded in life beyond my furthest dreams. Somewhere, somehow, I have developed a lot of resilience and resourcefulness. Was it *despite* my father? Or *because* of him?"

The fantasy was a first step in a major shift in her view of the past. It was not so much a question of forgiving her father but coming to terms with the inalterability of the past. She was shaken by my comment that sooner or later she had to give up the hope for a better past. She had been shaped and toughened by the adversity she faced at home; she learned how to cope with it and developed ingenious strategies that served her well throughout her life.

"Some Refuse the Loan of Life to Avoid the Debt of Death"

Bernice entered therapy with a vexing problem. Though she and her husband, Steve, had had a loving marriage for over twenty tears, she felt unaccountably irritated with him. She felt herself withdrawing to the point of entertaining fantasies of separation.

I wondered about the timing and asked when she had begun to change her feelings about Steve. She was precise in her answer: things started to go wrong on his seventieth birthday, when he suddenly retired from his job as a stockbroker and began managing his personal portfolio from home.

She was baffled by her anger at him. Though he had in no way changed, she now found myriad things to criticize: his messiness, his excessive TV time, his inattentiveness to his appearance, his lack of exercise. Though Steve was twenty-five years older than she, he had *always* been twenty-five years older. It was the marker of retirement that had made her aware that he was now an old man.

Several dynamics emerged from our discussion. First, she hoped to distance herself from Steve to avoid being, as she put it, "fast-forwarded" into old age. Second, she had never been able to erase the pain of her mother's death when she had been a child of ten; she did not want to have to face the reemergence of painful loss that would surely occur when Steve died.

It seemed to me that Bernice attempted to protect herself from the pain of losing Steve by lessening her attachment to him. I suggested that neither her anger nor her withdrawal seemed effective ways of avoiding endings and loss. I was able to make her own dynamics crystal clear to her by quoting Otto Rank, one of Freud's colleagues, who said, "Some refuse the loan of life to avoid the debt of death." This dynamic is not uncommon. I think most of us have known individuals who numb themselves and avoid entering life with gusto because of the dread of losing too much.

As we proceeded, I said, "It's like going on an ocean cruise and refusing to enter into friendships or interesting activities in order to avoid the pain of the inevitable end of the cruise."

"You got it exactly," she responded.

"Or not enjoying the sunrise because—"

"Yes, yes, yes, you've made your point," she laughed and interrupted.

As we settled down to the business of change, several themes emerged. She feared reopening the wound she had suffered at the age of ten when her mother died. After several sessions, she grew to understand the inefficiency of her unconscious strategy. First, she was no longer a helpless, resourceless ten-year-old child. Not only was it impossible to avoid grief when Steve died, but her grief would be greatly compounded by the guilt at having abandoned him when he most needed her.

Otto Rank posited a useful dynamic, an ongoing tension between "life anxiety" and "death anxiety," which may be exceedingly useful to the therapist. In his view, a developing person strives for individuation, growth, and fulfillment of his or her potential. But there is a cost! In emerging, expanding, and standing out from nature, an individual encounters life anxiety, a frightening loneliness, a feeling of vulnerability, a loss of basic connection with a greater whole. When this life anxiety becomes unbearable, what do we do? We take a different direction: we go backward; we retreat from separateness and find comfort in merger—that is, in fusing with and giving oneself up to the other.

Yet despite its comfort and coziness, the solution of merger is unstable: ultimately one recoils from the loss of the unique self and sense of stagnation. Thus, merger gives rise to "death anxiety." Between these two poles—life anxiety and death anxiety, or individuation and merger—people shuttle back and forth their entire lives. This formulation ultimately became the spine of

Ernest Becker's extraordinary book, *The Denial of Death*.

A few months after Bernice terminated therapy, she had a curious, highly unsettling nightmare and requested a consultation to discuss it. She described the dream in an e-mail:

I am terrified by an alligator chasing me. Though I am able to leap up twenty feet in the air to elude him, he keeps on coming. Wherever I try to hide he finds me. I wake up shivering and drenched with sweat.

In our session, she grappled with the meaning of the dream. She knew that the crocodile represented death pursuing her. She realized, too, that there was no escape. But why now? The answer became apparent when we explored the events of the day preceding the nightmare. That evening her husband, Steve, had narrowly avoided a serious automobile accident, and they subsequently had a terrible quarrel when she insisted that he give up night driving forever because of his impaired night vision.

But why a crocodile? Where had that come from? She recalled she had gone to bed that night after watching a disturbing TV news report about the horrifying death of Steve Irwin, the Australian "crocodile man" who had been killed by a stingray in a diving accident. As we continued to speak, she had an "aha" experience when she suddenly realized that the name Steve Irwin

was a combination of her husband's name and mine—
the two elderly men whose death she most dreaded.

SCHOPENHAUER'S TRIPLET OF ESSAYS: WHAT A MAN IS, WHAT A MAN HAS, WHAT A MAN REPRESENTS

Who among us has not known someone (including, perhaps, ourselves) so outwardly directed, so concerned about accumulating possessions or about what others think, as to lose all sense of self? Such a person, when posed a question, searches outward rather than inward for the answer; that is, he or she scans the faces of others to divine which answer they desire or expect.

For such a person, I find it useful to summarize a triplet of essays that Schopenhauer wrote late in life. (For anyone philosophically inclined, they are written in clear, accessible language.) Basically the essays emphasize that it is only what an individual *is* that counts; neither wealth nor material goods nor social status nor a good reputation results in happiness. Though these thoughts are not explicitly about existential issues, they nonetheless assist in moving us from superficial ground to deeper issues.

1. *What we have.* Material goods are a will-o'-the-wisp. Schopenhauer argues elegantly that the

accumulation of wealth and goods is endless and unsatisfying; the more we possess, the more our claims multiply. Wealth is like seawater: the more we drink, the thirstier we become. In the end, we don't have our goods—*they have us.*

2. *What we represent in the eyes of others.* Reputation is as evanescent as material wealth. Schopenhauer writes, "Half our worries and anxieties have arisen from our concern about the opinions of others . . . we must extract this thorn from our flesh." So powerful is the urge to create a good appearance that some prisoners have gone to their execution with their clothing and final gestures foremost in their thoughts. The opinion of others is a phantasm that may alter at any moment. Opinions hang by a thread and make us slaves to what others think or, worse, to *what they appear to think*—for we can never know what they actually think.

3. *What we are.* It is only what we are that truly matters. A good conscience, Schopenhauer says, means more than a good reputation. Our greatest goal should be good health and intellectual wealth, which lead to an inexhaustible supply of ideas, independence, and a moral life. Inner equanimity stems from knowing *that it is not things that disturb us, but our interpretations of things.*

This last idea—that the quality of our life is determined by how we interpret our experiences, not by the experiences themselves—is an important therapeutic doctrine dating back to antiquity. A central tenet in the school of Stoicism, it passed through Zeno, Seneca, Marcus Aurelius, Spinoza, Schopenhauer, and Nietzsche, to become a fundamental concept in both dynamic and cognitive-behavioral therapy.

———

Such ideas as the Epicurean arguments, rippling, the avoidance of the unlived life, and emphasis on authenticity in the aphorisms I cite all have usefulness in combating death anxiety. But the power of all these ideas is greatly enhanced by one other component—intimate connection to others—to which I turn in the next chapter.

Chapter 5

OVERCOMING DEATH TERROR THROUGH CONNECTION

When we finally know we are dying, and all other
sentient beings are dying with us, we start to have a
burning, almost heartbreaking sense of the fragility
and preciousness of each moment and each being,
and from this can grow a deep, clear, limitless
compassion for all beings.

SOGYAL RINPOCHE, *The Tibetan Book of Living and Dying*

Death is destiny. Your wish to survive and your
dread of annihilation will always be there. It's
instinctive—built into your protoplasm—and has a mo-
mentous effect on how you live.

Over the centuries, we humans have developed an
enormous array of methods—some conscious, some unconscious, perhaps as many as there are individuals—to

ameliorate the fear of death. Some methods work; some are shaky and inefficient. Of those people who permit themselves to encounter death authentically and to integrate its shadow into their core being, the young woman who wrote this e-mail is a prime example:

I lost my beloved father two years ago and I have experienced previously unimaginable growth since. Before then I'd often wondered about my own ability to confront my finiteness and had been haunted by the idea that I, too, will someday pass from this life. However, I have now found in those fears and anxieties a love for living I didn't know before. Sometimes I feel removed from my peers because I feel less concern about minor passing events and styles. However I can accept that because I feel I do have a firm grip on what is and is not of importance. I think I will have to learn to deal with the strain about doing the things that will enrich my life instead of the things society may expect of me. . . . 'Tis wonderful to know my reignited ambition is more than a cover-up of my fears of dying. It is, in fact, my own willingness to accept and acknowledge mortality. I guess that I have gained some real confidence in my ability to "get it."

Those who don't "get it" usually deal with mortality through denial, diversion, or displacement. We've seen examples of such inadequate coping in earlier vignettes: Julia, who was so chronically fearful that she refused to participate in any activity carrying even the slightest risk, and Susan, who displaced death anxiety onto minor concerns (see Chapter Three); and others who were haunted by nightmares, or who narrowed themselves, "refusing the loan of life to avoid the debt of death." Still others compulsively search for novelty, sex, endless wealth, or power.

Adults who are racked with death anxiety are not odd birds who have contracted some exotic disease, but men and women whose family and culture have failed to knit the proper protective clothing for them to withstand the icy chill of mortality. They might have encountered too much death at too early a stage of life; they may have failed to experience a center of love, caring, and safety in their home; they may have been isolated individuals who never shared their intimate mortal concerns; they may have been hypersensitive, particularly self-aware individuals who have rejected the comfort of death-denying religious myths proffered by their culture.

Every historical era develops its own methods of dealing with death. Many cultures—for example, ancient Egypt—were explicitly organized around the denial of death and the promise of life after death. The tombs of the dead—at least, the upper-class ones (which are the ones that survive)—were filled with artifacts of everyday life that would make for a cozier afterlife.

To cite one quirky example, the Brooklyn Museum of Art contains funerary statues of hippopotamuses that were interred with the dead for their amusement in the afterlife. Lest, however, these stone animals frighten the dead, they were given such short legs as to be slow and thereby harmless.

In European and Western culture in the more recent past, death was more visible because of the high mortality rate of children and women in childbirth. The dying were not sequestered in a curtained hospital bed as they are today; instead most people died at home, with family members present at their final moment. Virtually no family was untouched by untimely death, and cemeteries were located, and frequently visited, at the graveyard near one's home. Because Christianity promises eternal afterlife, and the clergy held official keys to life's entrance and exit, most of the populace turned to religious consolation that usually contained the promise of an afterlife. And, of course, many people derive comfort from those beliefs today. In my discussion of religious consolation in Chapter Six, I'll try to distinguish between consolation in the face of death's finality and consolation through the denial, or de-deathification, of death.

For me, personally and in my practice of psychotherapy, the most effective approach to death anxiety is the existential one. Thus far, I've outlined a number of powerful ideas that have intrinsic value, but in this chapter I want to discuss an additional component required to make the ideas truly mutative: human connectedness. It is the synergy between ideas and intimate connection with other people that is most effective both in diminishing death anxiety and in harnessing the awakening experience to effect personal change.

HUMAN CONNECTEDNESS

We human beings are all hardwired to connect with others. From whatever perspective we study human society, whether its broad evolutionary history or the development of a single individual, we are obliged to view the human being in his or her interpersonal context—as related to others. There is convincing data from the study of nonhuman primates, primitive human cultures, and contemporary society that our need to belong is powerful and fundamental: we have always lived in groups with intense and persistent relationships among members. Confirmation is ubiquitous: to cite only one example, many recent studies in positive psychology stress that intimate relationships are a sine qua non for happiness.

Dying, however, is lonely, the loneliest event of life. Dying not only separates you from others but also exposes you to a second, even more frightening form of loneliness: separation from the world itself.

Two Kinds of Loneliness

There are two kinds of loneliness: everyday and existential. The former is interpersonal, the pain of being isolated from other people. This loneliness—often connected with fear of intimacy or feelings of rejection, shame, or being unlovable—is familiar to all of us. In fact, most of the work in psychotherapy is directed toward helping clients learn to form more intimate, sustaining, and enduring relationships with others.

Loneliness greatly increases the anguish of dying. Too often, our culture creates a curtain of silence and isolation around the dying. In the presence of the dying, friends and family members often grow more distant because they don't know what to say. They fear upsetting the dying person. And they also avoid getting too close for fear of personally confronting their own death. Even the Greek gods fled in fear when the moment of human death approached.

This everyday isolation works two ways: not only do the well tend to avoid the dying, but the dying often collude in their isolation. They embrace silence lest they drag people they love down into their macabre, despondent world. A person who is not physically ill, but in the midst of death anxiety, can feel much the same. Such isolation, of course, compounds the terror. As William James wrote a century ago, "No more fiendish punishment could be devised, were such a thing physically possible, than that one should be turned loose in society and remain absolutely unnoticed by all the members thereof."

The second form of loneliness, existential isolation, is more profound and stems from the unbridgeable gap between the individual and other people. This gap is a consequence not only of each of us having been thrown alone into existence and having to exit alone, but derives from the fact that each of us inhabits a world fully known only to ourselves.

In the eighteenth century, Immanuel Kant exploded the prevailing, commonsense assumption that we all enter and inhabit a finished, well-constructed, shared world. Today, we know that owing to our neurological apparatus, each person plays a substantial role in the creation of his or her own reality. In other words, you have a number of inbuilt mental categories (for example, quantity, quality, and cause and effect) that come into play when you confront incoming sense data and that enable you to automatically and unconsciously constitute the world in a unique manner.

Thus existential isolation refers to the loss not only of your biological life but also of your own rich, miraculously detailed world, which does not exist in the same manner in the mind of anyone else. My own poignant memories—burying my face into the musty, slight camphor odor of my mother's Persian lamb coat, the glances full of exciting possibility exchanged with girls on Valentine's Day in elementary school, playing chess with my father and pinochle with my uncles on a table with a red leather top and ebony curved legs, building a fireworks stand with my cousin when I was twenty— all these memories, and others more numerous than the stars in the heavens, are available only to me. And each and every one is but a ghostly image and will be switched off forever with my death.

Each of us experiences interpersonal isolation (the everyday feeling of loneliness) in varying fashion during all phases of the life cycle. But *existential isolation* is less common early in life; one experiences it most keenly when one is older and closer to death. At such times, we grow aware of the fact that our world will disappear and aware, too, that no one can fully accompany us on our bleak journey to death. As the old spiritual reminds us, "You got to walk that lonesome valley by yourself."

History and mythology are replete with people's attempts to mitigate the isolation of dying. Think of suicide pacts, or of monarchs in many cultures who ordered slaves to be buried alive with them, or the Indian practice of *sati,* requiring a widow to be immolated on the funeral pyre of her husband. Think of heavenly reunion and resurrection. Think of Socrates' absolute certainty that he would spend eternity conversing with other great-minded thinkers. Think of the Chinese peasant culture—to cite a recent singular example in the parched canyons in the Loess Plateau—in which parents with dead bachelor sons will purchase a dead woman (from those who dig up graves or locate a new corpse) and bury the pair together as a couple.

Cries and Whispers: The Power of Empathy

Empathy is the most powerful tool we have in our efforts to connect with other people. It is the glue of human connectedness and permits us to feel, at a deep level, what someone else is feeling.

Nowhere is the loneliness of death and the need for connectedness depicted more graphically and powerfully than in Ingmar Bergman's masterpiece *Cries and Whispers*. In the film, Agnes, a woman dying in great pain and terror, pleads for some intimate human touch. Her two sisters are deeply affected by Agnes's dying. One sister is awakened to the realization that her own life has been a "tissue of lies." But neither can bring herself to touch Agnes. Neither has the ability to be intimate with anyone, even themselves, and both shrink away in terror from their dying sister. Only Anna, the housemaid, is willing to hold Agnes, flesh to flesh.

Shortly after Agnes dies, her lonely spirit returns and pleads, in the eerie wailing voice of a young child, for her sisters' touch, which will permit her to truly die. The two sisters attempt to come closer but, terrified by the mottled skin of death and by the prevision of their own awaiting death, flee in horror from the room. Once again, it is Anna's embrace that enables Agnes to complete the journey into death.

You can't connect or offer the dying what Anna does in this film unless you're willing to face your own equivalent fears and join with the other on common ground. To make that sacrifice for the other is the essence of a truly compassionate, empathic act. This willingness to experience one's own pain in concert with another has been a part of the healing traditions, both secular and religious, for centuries.

It is not easy to do this. Like Agnes's sisters, family members or close friends may be eager to help but are too timid; people may fear that they are intruding or that they will unsettle the dying by raising somber topics. The dying person generally needs to take the lead in discussing fears about death. If you are dying or panicky about death, and your friends and family remain distant or respond evasively, I would suggest you stay in the here-and-now (to be discussed more fully in Chapter Seven) and speak directly to the point—for example: "I notice you don't respond directly when I discuss my fears. It will help me if I can speak openly to close friends like you. Is it too much, too painful, for you?"

Today there is much greater opportunity for all of us who experience death anxiety, in whatever form, to connect not only with our loved ones but with a larger community. With the greater openness in medicine and in the media, and with the availability of groups, the person facing death has new resources to temper the pain of isolation. Today most good cancer centers, for example, offer patient support groups. Yet only thirty-five years ago, the group I formed for terminally ill cancer patients was, as far as I know, the first such group in the world.

Moreover, the use of Internet support groups of all varieties is dramatically escalating: a recent survey indicated that in a single year, fifteen million people had sought help from some form of online group. I urge anyone who has a life-threatening disease to take advantage of groups composed of individuals suffering from a similar condition. Such groups, whether self-help or led by professionals, are easily found.

The most effective group is usually led by a professional. Research demonstrates that leader-led groups of people who are similarly afflicted improve the quality of participants' lives. In offering empathy to one another, the members increase their own self-regard and sense of efficacy. Recent research also attests, however, to the efficacy of self-help and online groups, so if a professionally led group is not available, seek out one of these.

THE POWER OF PRESENCE

One can offer no greater service to someone facing death (and from this point on I speak either of those suffering from a fatal illness or physically healthy individuals experiencing death terror) than to offer him or her your sheer presence.

The following vignette, which describes my attempt to assuage a woman's death terror, provides guidelines to friends or family members offering aid to one another.

Reaching Out to Friends: Alice

Alice—the widow whose story I told in Chapter Three, who was distressed at having to sell her home and her memory-laden collection of musical instruments—was on the verge of moving into a retirement community. Shortly before her move, I left town for a few days' vacation and, knowing this would be a difficult time for her, gave her my cell phone number in case of an emergency. As the movers began to empty her house, Alice experienced a paralyzing panic that her friends, physician, and massage therapist could not quell. She phoned me, and we had a twenty-minute talk:

"I can't sit still," she began. "I'm so edgy I feel I'm going to burst. I cannot find relief."

"Look straight into the heart of your panic. Tell me what you see."

"Ending. Everything ending. That's all. The end of my house, all my things, my memories, my attachments to my past. The end of everything. The end of me—that's the heart of it. You want to know what I fear. It's simple: *it's no more me!*"

"We've discussed this in other meetings, Alice, so I know I'm repeating myself, but I want to remind you that selling your house and moving to a retirement home is an extraordinary trauma, and *of course* you're going to feel major dislocation and major shock. I would feel that way if I were in your place. Anyone would. But remember our talks about how it will look if you fast-forward to three weeks from now—"

"Irv," she interrupted, "that doesn't help—this pain is too raw. This is death surrounding me. Death everywhere. I want to scream."

"Bear with me, Alice. Stay with me—I'm going to ask that same simplistic question I've asked before: what precisely is it about death that so frightens you? Let's hone in on it."

"We've gone over this." Alice sounded irritated and impatient.

"Not enough. Keep going, Alice. Humor me, please. Come on, let's get to work."

"Well, it's not the pain of dying. I trust my oncologist; he will be there when I need morphine or something. And it has nothing to do with an afterlife—you know I let go of all that stuff a half century ago."

"So it's not the act of dying and not the fear of an afterlife. Keep going. What *is* it about death that terrifies you?"

"It's not that I feel unfinished; I know I've had a full life. I've done what I've wanted to do. We've gone over all this."

"Please keep going, Alice."

"It's what I just said: *no more me.* I just don't want to leave this life . . . I'll tell you what it is: I want to see the endings. I want to be here to see what happens to my son—will he decide to have children after all. It's painful to realize I won't ever be able to know."

"But you won't know you're not here. You won't know you won't know. You say you believe (as I do) that death is complete cessation of consciousness."

"I know, I know, you've said it so many times that I know the whole litany by heart: *the state of nonexistence is not terrifying because we won't know we are not existing,* and so on and so on. And that means I won't know that I am missing important things. And I remember also what you've already said about the state of nonbeing—that it's identical to the state I was in before I was born. It helped before, but it just doesn't help now—this feeling is too strong, Irv—ideas won't crack it; they won't even touch it."

"Not yet they won't. That only means we have to keep going, keep figuring it out. We can do it together. I'll be in there with you and help you go as deep as you can."

"It's gripping terror. There is some menace I cannot name or find."

"Alice, at the very base of all our feelings about death there is a biological fear that is hardwired into us. I know this fear is inchoate—I've experienced it too. It doesn't have words. But every living creature wishes to persist in its own being—Spinoza said that around 350 years ago. We just have to know this, expect it. The hardwiring will zap us with terror from time to time. We all have it."

After about twenty minutes, Alice sounded calmer, and we ended the call. A few hours later, however, she left a curt phone message telling me that the phone session felt like a slap in the face and that I was cold and unempathic. Almost as a postscript she added that, unaccountably, she felt better. The following day she left another message saying that her panic had entirely subsided—again, she said, for reasons unknown.

Now, why was Alice helped by this conversation? Was it the ideas I presented? Probably not. She dismissed my arguments from Epicurus—that, with her consciousness extinguished, she wouldn't know that she'd never find out how the stories of people close to her ended, and that after death she would be in the same state as she was before her birth. Nor did any of my other suggestions—for example, that she project herself three weeks into the future to gain some perspective on her life—have any impact whatsoever. She was simply too panicky. As she put it, "I know you're trying, but these ideas won't crack it; they don't even touch what's here—this anguished heaviness in my chest."

So ideas didn't help. But let's examine the conversation from the perspective of relationship. First, I spoke to her on my vacation, thereby indicating my full willingness to be involved with her. I said, in effect, let's you and I keep working on this together. I didn't shrink from any aspect of her anxiety. I continued inquiring into her feelings about death. I acknowledged my own anxiety. I assured her that we were in this together, that she and I and everyone else are hardwired to feel anxious about death.

Second, behind my explicit offer of presence, there was a strong *implicit* message: "No matter how much terror you have, I will never shun or abandon you." I was simply doing what the housemaid, Anna, did in *Cries and Whispers.* I held her, stayed with her.

Although I felt fully involved with her, I made sure that I kept her terror contained. I did not permit it to be contagious. I maintained an unruffled, matter-of-fact tone as I urged her to join me in dissecting and analyzing the terror. Although she criticized me the following day for being cold and unempathic, my calmness nonetheless steadied her and helped allay her terror.

The lesson here is simple: *connection is paramount.* Whether you are a family member, a friend, or a therapist, jump in. Get close in any way that feels appropriate. Speak from your heart. Reveal your own fears. Improvise. Hold the suffering one in any way that gives comfort.

Once, decades ago, as I was saying goodbye to a patient near death, she asked me to lie next to her on her bed for a while. I did as she requested and, I believe, offered her comfort. Sheer presence is the greatest gift you can offer anyone facing death (or a physically healthy person in a death panic).

SELF-DISCLOSURE

A great deal of a therapist's training, as I'll discuss in Chapter Seven, focuses on the centrality of connection. An essential part of that training should, in my opinion, focus on the therapist's willingness and ability to increase connection through his or her own transparency.

Because many therapists have trained in traditions that stress the importance of opaqueness and neutrality, friends willing to reveal themselves to one another may, in this regard, have an advantage over professional therapists.

In close relationships, the more one reveals of one's inner feelings and thoughts, the easier it is for others to reveal themselves. Self-disclosure plays a crucial role in the development of intimacy. Generally, relationships build by a process of reciprocal self-revelations. One individual takes the leap and reveals some intimate material, thereby placing himself or herself at risk; the other closes the gap by reciprocating in kind; together, they deepen the relationship via a spiral of self-revelation. If the person at risk is left hanging without the other reciprocating, then the friendship often flounders.

The more you can be truly yourself, can share yourself fully, the deeper and more sustaining the friendship. In the presence of such intimacy, all words, all modes of comfort, and all ideas take on greater meaning.

Friends must keep reminding one another (and themselves) that they, too, experience the fear of death. Thus, in my conversation with Alice, I included myself in discussions of death's inevitability. Such disclosure is not high risk: it is merely making explicit what is implicit. After all, we are all creatures who are frightened at the thought of "no more me." We all face the sense of our smallness and insignificance when measured against the infinite extent of the universe (sometimes referred to as the "experience of the tremendum"). Each of us is but a speck, a grain of sand, in the vastness of the cosmos. As Pascal said in the seventeenth century, "the eternal silence of infinite spaces terrifies me."

The need for intimacy in the face of death is heart-breakingly described in a recent rehearsal of a new play, *Let Me Down Easy,* by Anna Deavere Smith. In this play, one of the characters portrayed was a remarkable woman who cared for African children with AIDS. Little help was available at her shelter. Children died every day. When asked what she did to ease the dying children's terror, she answered with two phrases: "I never let them die alone in the dark, and I say to them, 'You will always be with me here in my heart.'"

Even for those with a deeply ingrained block against openness—those who have always avoided deep friendships—the idea of death may be an awakening experience, catalyzing an enormous shift in their desire for intimacy and their willingness to make efforts to attain it. Many people who work with dying patients have found that those who were previously distant become strikingly and suddenly accessible to deep engagement.

RIPPLING IN ACTION

As I explained in the previous chapter, the belief that one may persist, not in one's individual personhood, but through values and actions that ripple on and on through generations to come can be a powerful consolation to anyone anxious about his or her mortality.

Alleviating the Loneliness of Death

Although *Everyman,* the medieval morality play, dramatizes the loneliness of one's encounter with death, it may also be read as portraying the consoling power of rippling. A theatrical crowd pleaser for centuries, *Everyman* played in front of churches before large throngs of parishioners. It tells the allegorical tale of Everyman, who is visited by the angel of death and learns that the time of his final journey has arrived.

Everyman pleads for a reprieve. "Nothing doing," replies the angel of death. Then another request: "Can I invite someone to accompany me on this desperately lonely journey?" The angel grins and readily agrees: "Oh, yes—if you can find someone."

The remainder of the play consists of Everyman's attempts to recruit someone to be his companion on the journey. Every friend and acquaintance declines; his cousin, for example, is indisposed by a cramp in her toe. Even metaphorical figures (Worldly Goods, Beauty, Strength, Knowledge) refuse his invitation. Finally, as he resigns himself to his lonely journey, he discovers one companion, Good Deeds, who is available and willing to accompany him, even unto death.

Everyman's discovery that there is one companion, Good Deeds, who is able to accompany him is, of course, the Christian moral of this morality play: that you can take with you from this world nothing that you have received; you can take only what you have given. A secular interpretation of this drama suggests that rippling—that is, the realization of your good deeds, of your virtuous influence on others that persists beyond yourself—may soften the pain and loneliness of the final journey.

The Role of Gratitude

Rippling, like so many of the ideas I find useful, assumes far more power in the context of an intimate relationship where one can know at first hand how one's life has benefited someone else.

Friends may thank someone for what he or she has done or meant. But mere thanks is not the point.

The truly effective message is, "I have taken some part of you into me. It has changed and enriched me, and I shall pass it on to others."

Far too often, gratitude for how a person has sent influential ripples out into the world is expressed not when the person is still alive but only in a posthumous eulogy. How many times at funerals have you wished (or overheard others express the wish) that the dead person were there to hear the eulogies and expressions of gratitude? How many of us have wished we could be like Scrooge and eavesdrop on our own funeral? I have.

One technique for overcoming this "too little, too late" problem with rippling is the "gratitude visit," a splendid way to enhance rippling when one is alive. I first came upon this exercise at a workshop conducted by Martin Seligman, one of the leaders of the positive psychology movement. He asked a large audience to participate in an exercise that, as I recall, went along these lines:

Think of someone still living toward whom you feel great gratitude that you have never expressed. Spend ten minutes writing that person a gratitude letter and then pair up with someone here, and each of you read your letter to the other. The final step is that you pay a personal visit to that person sometime in the near future and read that letter aloud.

After the letters were read in pairs, several volunteers were selected from the audience to read their letters aloud to the entire audience. Without exception, each person choked up with emotion during the reading. I learned that such displays of emotion invariably occur in this exercise: very few participants get through the reading without being swept by a deep emotional current.

I did the exercise myself and wrote such a letter to David Hamburg, who had been a superbly enabling chairman of the Department of Psychiatry during my first ten years at Stanford. When I next visited New York, where he lived at this time, we spent a moving evening together. I felt good expressing my gratitude, and he felt good about knowing of it; he said he had beamed with pleasure when reading my letter.

As I age, I think more and more about rippling. As a paterfamilias, I always pick up the check when my family dines at a restaurant. My four children always thank me graciously (after offering only feeble resistance), and I always say to them, "Thank your grandfather Ben Yalom. I'm only a vessel passing on his generosity. He always picked up the check for me." (And I, by the way, also offered only feeble resistance.)

Rippling and Modeling

In the first group I led for patients with terminal cancer, I often found the members' despondency contagious. So many members were in despair; so many waited day after day listening for the approaching footsteps of death; so many claimed that life had become empty and stripped of all meaning.

And then, one fine day, a member opened our meeting with an announcement: "I have decided that there is, after all, something that I can still offer. I can offer an example of how to die. I can set a model for my children and my friends by facing death with courage and dignity."

It was a revelation that lifted her spirits, and mine, and those of the other members of the group. She had found a way to imbue her life, to its very end, with meaning.

The phenomenon of rippling was evident in the cancer group members' attitude toward student observers. It is vital for the education of group therapists that they observe experienced clinicians leading groups, and I have usually had students observing my groups, sometimes using TV monitors but generally through a one-way mirror. Although groups in educational settings give permission for such observation, the group members generally grumble about the observers and, from time to time, openly voice resentment at the intrusion.

Not so with my groups of cancer patients: they welcomed observers. They felt that as a result of their confrontation with death, they had grown wise and had much to pass on to students and regretted only, as I mentioned earlier, that they had waited so long to learn how to live.

Discovering Your Own Wisdom

Socrates believed that the best course for a teacher—
and, let me add, a friend—is to ask questions that will
help a student excavate his or her own wisdom.
Friends do this all the time, as do therapists. The following vignette illustrates a simple device available to
all of us.

If We Are Going to Die, Then Why or How Should We Live?: Jill

Again and again people ask, What is the purpose of life
if all is destined to vanish? Though many of us search
for the answer to this question outside ourselves, you
would do better to follow the method of Socrates and
turn your gaze within.

Jill, a patient who had long been plagued with
death anxiety, habitually equated death and meaninglessness. When I asked her for a history of the development of this thought, she recalled vividly its first
appearance. Closing her eyes, she described a scene
when she was nine years old sitting on her front porch
glider and grieving the death of the family's dog.

"Then and there," she said, "I realized that if we
must all die, nothing had any point—my piano lessons,
my making my bed perfectly, my gold stars at school

for perfect attendance. What's the point of gold stars when all gold stars will vanish?"

"Jill," I said, "you have a young daughter who's about nine. Imagine that she asked, 'If we are going to die, then why or how should we live?' How would you answer?"

Unhesitatingly she replied, "I'd tell her about the many joys of living, the beauty of the forests, the pleasure of being with friends and family, the bliss of spreading love to others and of leaving the world a better place."

After finishing, she leaned back in her chair and opened her eyes wide, astonished at her own words, as though to say, "Where did *that* come from?"

"Great answer, Jill. You've got so much wisdom inside. This is not the first time you've arrived at a great truth when you imagine advising your daughter about life. Now you need to learn to be your own mother."

The task, then, is not to offer answers, but to find a way to help others discover their own answers.

The same principle operated in the treatment of Julia, the psychotherapist and painter, whose death anxiety stemmed from her not having fully realized herself and neglecting her art in order to compete with her husband in earning money (see Chapter Three). I applied the same strategy in our work when I asked her to assume a distant perspective by suggesting she imagine how she'd respond to a client who behaved as she did.

Julia's instantaneous comment—"I'd say to her, *you are living a life of absurdity!*"—signaled that she needed only the slightest guidance to discover her own wisdom. Therapists have always operated under the assumption that the truth one discovers for oneself has far greater power than a truth delivered by others.

FULFILLING YOUR LIFE

The death anxiety of many people is fueled, as it was for Julia, by disappointment at never having fulfilled their potential. Many people are in despair because their dreams didn't come true, and they despair even more that they did not make them come true. A focus on this deep dissatisfaction is often the starting point in overcoming death anxiety, as in Jack's story:

Death Anxiety and the Unlived Life: Jack

Jack, a tall, well-dressed sixty-year-old attorney, came to my office wracked with disabling symptoms. He told me in a rather flat, inexpressive tone that he was having obsessive thoughts about death, that he couldn't sleep, and that he was suffering from a dramatic decline in professional productivity that had reduced his income substantially. He frittered away hours each week compulsively consulting actuarial tables and calculating the likely months and days remaining in his life. Two or three times a week he was awakened by nightmares.

His income had dropped because he could no longer deal with the wills and estate law that were a large part of his practice: so fixated was he on his own will and his own death that imminent panic often forced him to cut consultations short. In conferences with clients, he embarrassed himself by stammering, sometimes actually gagging, over words like "predecease," "passing on," "surviving spouse," and "death benefits."

During our first sessions, Jack seemed remote and guarded. I tried many of the ideas I've described in this book to reach him or offer comfort, but without success. One odd thing caught my attention: three of the dreams he described involved cigarettes. For example, in one dream he was walking through an underground passage littered with cigarettes. Yet he said he had not smoked in twenty-five years. When I pressed him for associations to cigarettes, he offered none until, at the very end of the third session, he revealed in a tremulous voice that his wife of forty years had smoked marijuana during every single day of their marriage. He put his head in his hands, fell silent, and, as the second hand on his watch signaled the end of fifty minutes, he bolted out the door without a goodbye comment.

In the next session, he spoke of his great shame. It was painful for him to admit that he, a well-educated, intelligent, respected professional, was stupid enough to stay in a relationship for forty years with an addict who showed cognitive impairment and whose grooming was so poor that it was an embarrassment to be seen with her in public.

Jack was shaken but, by the end of the session, felt relieved. He had revealed this secret to no one all these years; in some strange way, he had hardly admitted it to himself.

In future sessions, he acknowledged that he had settled for an impaired relationship because he didn't believe he deserved more, and acknowledged the far-reaching ramifications of his marriage. His shame and need for secrecy had eliminated any other social life. He had decided to have no children: his wife was incapable of abstinence during pregnancy or of being a responsible role model for children. So convinced was he that he would be considered a fool for remaining with her, he had not confided in anyone, not even his sister.

Now, at the age of sixty, he was firmly persuaded that he was too old and too isolated to leave his wife. He made it crystal clear to me that any discussion of ending, or threatening to end, his marriage was off-limits. Despite his wife's addiction, he genuinely loved her, needed her, and took his marital vows seriously. He knew that she could not live without him.

I realized that his death anxiety was related to his having only partially lived and having stifled his own dreams for happiness and fulfillment. His terror and nightmares flowed from his sense that time was running out, his life slipping away.

I was particularly struck by his isolation. The need for secrecy had precluded any intimate relationship other than the troubled and ambivalent one with his wife. I approached his intimacy problems by focusing on our relationship and started by making it clear I would never judge him a fool. Instead, I felt honored that he had been willing to share so much with me, and I empathized with him for the moral predicament he faced in living with an impaired spouse.

After only a few such sessions, Jack's death anxiety diminished markedly. It was replaced by other concerns, primarily his relationship with his wife and the ways in which his shame precluded other intimate connections. We brainstormed together about how he might proceed to break the code of secrecy that had obstructed him from forming other friendships all these years. I raised the possibility of a therapy group, but that seemed far too threatening: he rejected the idea of any ambitious therapy that might disrupt his relationship with his wife. Instead he identified two individuals, his sister and a man who had once been a close friend, with whom he would share his secret.

I made a point of focusing on the issue of self-fulfillment. What were the stifled parts of himself that could yet be realized? What were his daydreams? As a child, what had he imagined doing in life? What endeavors in the past gave him the deepest pleasure?

He arrived at the next session holding a thick binder filled with what he called his "doodles"—decades of poetry, often about death, much of it written at four in the morning when he was awakened by a nightmare. I asked if he would read some to me, and he selected three of his favorites.

"How wonderful," I told him when he finished, "to be able to turn your despair into something so beautiful."

After twelve sessions, Jack reported that he had achieved his goals: his terror of death had markedly diminished; his nightmares had morphed into dreams with only thin slivers of irritation or frustration. His revealing himself to me gave him the courage to trust others, and he restored a close relationship with his sister and his old friend. Three months later he e-mailed me that he was doing fine and had enrolled in an online writing seminar and joined a local poetry writing group.

My work with Jack demonstrates how a stifled life may express itself as death terror. *Of course* he was in terror: he had much to fear from death because he had not lived the life available to him. Legions of artists and writers have expressed this sentiment in a multiplicity of tongues, from Nietzsche's "Die at the right time" to the American poet John Greenleaf Whittier's "For of all sad words of tongue or pen, the saddest are these: 'It might have been!'"

My work with Jack was also sprinkled with attempts to help him locate and revitalize neglected parts of himself, ranging from his poetic gifts to his thirst for an intimate social network. Therapists realize that it is generally better to try to help a client remove the obstacles to self-actualization than to rely on suggestions or encouragement or exhortation.

I also tried to reduce Jack's isolation, not by pointing out the social opportunities available to him, but instead by focusing on the major obstacles to intimate friendships: his shame and belief that others would regard him as a foolish man. And, of course, his leap into intimacy with me was a major step: isolation only exists in isolation; once shared, it evaporates.

The Value of Regret

Regret has been given a bad name. Although it usually connotes irredeemable sadness, it can be used in a constructive manner. In fact, of all the methods I use to help myself and others examine self-realization, the idea of regret—both creating and avoiding it—is most valuable.

Properly used, regret is a tool that can help you take actions to prevent its further accumulation. You can examine regret both by looking behind and by looking ahead. If you turn your gaze toward the past, you experience regret for all that you have not fulfilled. If you turn your gaze to the future, you experience the possibility of either amassing more regret or living relatively free of it.

I often counsel myself and my patients to imagine one year or five years ahead and think of the new regrets that will have piled up in that period. Then I pose a question that has real therapeutic crunch: "How can you live now without building new regrets? What do you have to change in your life?"

WAKING UP

At some point in life—sometimes in youth, sometimes late—each of us is due to awaken to our mortality. There are so many triggers: a glance in a mirror at your sagging jowls, graying hair, stooping shoulders; the march of birthdays, especially those round decades—fifty, sixty, seventy; meeting a friend you have not seen in a long while and being shocked at how he or she has aged; seeing old photographs of yourself and those long dead who peopled your childhood; encountering Mister Death in a dream.

What do you *feel* when you have such experiences? What do you *do* with them? Do you plunge into frenetic activity to burn off the anxiety and avoid the subject? Try to remove wrinkles with cosmetic surgery or dye your hair? Decide to stay thirty-nine for a few more years? Distract yourself quickly with work and everyday life routine? Forget all such experiences? Ignore your dreams?

I urge you not to distract yourself. Instead, savor awakening. Take advantage of it. Pause as you stare into the photograph of the younger you. Let the poignant moment sweep over you and linger a bit; taste the sweetness of it as well as the bitterness.

Keep in mind the advantage of remaining aware of death, of hugging its shadow to you. Such awareness can integrate the darkness with your spark of life and enhance your life while you still have it. *The way to value life, the way to feel compassion for others, the way to love anything with greatest depth is to be aware that these experiences are destined to be lost.*

Many times I've been pleasantly surprised to see a patient make substantial positive changes very late in life, even close to death. It's never too late. You're never too old.

Chapter 6

DEATH AWARENESS

A Memoir

———

For, as I draw closer and closer to the end, I travel in a circle nearer and nearer to the beginning. It seems to be one of the kind of smoothings and preparings of the way. My heart is touched now by many remembrances that had long fallen asleep.
CHARLES DICKENS, *A Tale of Two Cities*

Nietzsche once commented that if you want to understand a philosopher's work, you have to examine his autobiography. So too with psychiatrists. It is common knowledge that in a wide range of endeavors, from quantum physics to economics, psychology, and sociology, the observer influences what is observed. I have presented my observations about my patients' lives and thoughts, and now it is time to reverse the

process and reveal my personal ideas about death—
their sources and how they have affected my life.

DEATHS FACED

So far as I remember, my first encounter with death was
at the age of five or six when Stripy, one of the cats my
father kept in his grocery store, was hit by a car. As I
watched her lying on the pavement, a thin ribbon of
blood trickling from her mouth, I put a marble-size piece
of hamburger next to her mouth, but she took no note:
she had appetite only for death. Unable to do anything
for Stripy, as I recall, I felt a numbing impotence. I don't
remember drawing the obvious conclusion that if all
other living creatures die, then so must I. However, the
details of my cat's death persist with preternatural clarity.

My first experience with a human death occurred
in the second or third grade with the death of a classmate named L. C. I don't recall what the initials stood
for; maybe I never knew—I'm not even sure we were
close friends or played together. All I have left are a few
radiant slivers of memory. L. C. was an albino with red
eyes, and his mother packed his lunch pail with sandwiches containing pickle slices. I thought that odd—
never before had I seen pickles inhabiting sandwiches.

Then one day L. C. stopped coming to school,
and after a week the teacher told us that he had died.

That was all. No further words. No mention of him, ever again. Like a shrouded body slipping from the deck into the dark sea, he silently vanished. But how clear he remains in my mind. Nearly seventy years have passed, yet I can almost reach out and run my fingers through his shock of stiff, ghost-white hair. As though I saw him yesterday, his image is fixed in my mind, and I see his white skin, high-laced shoes, and, above all, that wide-eyed look of absolute astonishment on his face. Perhaps it's all a reconstruction; perhaps I simply imagine how astonished he must have been to have met Mister Death at such an early point in his life journey.

"Mister Death" is a term I have used since I was a young adolescent. I picked it up from an E. E. Cummings poem about Buffalo Bill, which so stunned me that I memorized it on the spot.

> *Buffalo Bill's*
> *defunct*
>> *who used to*
>> *ride a watersmooth-silver*
>>> *stallion*
> *and break onetwothreefourfive pigeonsjustlikethat*
>>>> *Jesus*
> *he was a handsome man*
>>> *and what i want to know is*
> *how do you like your blueeyed boy*
> *Mister Death*

I don't remember having much emotion about L. C.'s vanishing. Freud wrote about our stripping unpleasant emotion from memory. That fits for me and clarifies the paradox of my obliterated emotion coupled with vivid imagery. I believe it's reasonable to infer that I had plenty of emotion about the death of a peer: it is no accident that I remember L. C. so clearly yet have retained not an image, not a scrap, of any other classmate from those early days. Perhaps, then, the sharpness of his image is all that is left from my staggering realization that I, my teachers, my classmates, all of us would sooner or later vanish like L. C.

Perhaps the E. E. Cummings poem set up permanent residence in my mind because during my adolescence, Mister Death visited another boy I knew. Allen Marinoff was a "blueeyed boy" who had a heart defect and was always ailing. I remember his pointed melancholic face, his wisps of light brown hair that he flicked back with his fingertips when they drooped over his forehead, his battered school book satchel, so incongruously large and heavy for his frail body. One evening when I slept over at his house, I tried—not too hard, I think—to ask what was wrong. "What is happening to you, Allen? What does it mean to have a hole in your heart?" It was all too terrible. Like staring into the sun. I don't recall how he answered. I don't recall what I felt or thought. But surely there were forces rumbling inside me, like heavy furniture being moved around, that resulted in such selective memory. Allen was fifteen when he died.

Unlike many children, I had no exposure to death at funerals; in my parents' culture, the young were excluded from such events. But something big happened when I was nine or ten. One evening the phone rang, and my father answered and almost immediately broke out into a loud, shrill wailing that frightened me. His brother, my Uncle Meyer, had died. Unable to bear my father's keening, I ran outside and raced again and again around the block.

My father was a quiet, gentle man, and this shocking, singular loss of all control signaled that something huge, portentous, monstrous lurked out there. My sister, seven years older, was home at the time and remembers none of this, though she recalls much that I do not. Such is the power of repression, that exquisitely selective process that—in determining what one remembers, what one forgets—is instrumental in constructing the unique personal world of each of us.

My father almost died from a coronary when he was forty-six. It happened in the middle of the night. I, fourteen years old, was terrified, and my mother was so distraught that she cast about for some explanation, someone to blame for this stroke of fate. I was the available target, and she let me know that I—with my unruliness, my disrespect, my disruption of the household—was wholly responsible for this catastrophe.

More than once that evening, as my father writhed with pain, she screamed at me, "You've killed him!"

Twelve years later, when I was on the analytic couch, my description of this event resulted in an unusual momentary outburst of tenderness from Olive Smith, my ultra-orthodox Freudian psychoanalyst, who clucked her tongue, tsk, tsk, as she leaned toward me and said, "How awful. How terrible that must have been for you." Of her thoughtful, dense, and carefully worded interpretations, I remember nary a one. But her reaching out in that caring moment—*that* I cherish even now, almost fifty years later. That night, my mother, my father, and I waited desperately for Dr. Manchester to arrive. Finally I heard his car crunching the autumn leaves in the street and flew downstairs three steps at a time to open the door. The familiar blessed sight of his large, round, smiling face dissolved my panic. He put his hand on my head, tousled my hair, reassured my mother, gave my father an injection (probably morphine), held his stethoscope to my father's chest, and let me listen as he said, "See, ticking away, regular as a clock. He's going to be all right."

That was a life-changing evening for me in many ways, but mostly I recall my ineffable relief at Dr. Manchester's entrance into our home. Then and there I decided to be like him, to be a physician and to pass on to others the comfort he had given me.

My father survived that night, but twenty years later he died suddenly in front of our entire family. I was visiting my sister in Washington, D.C., with my wife and three young children. He and my mother had driven over; he sat down in the living room, complained of a headache, and suddenly collapsed.

My sister's husband, also a physician, was stunned. Later he said that in his thirty years of practice he had never before witnessed the instant of death. Without losing my cool, I pounded on my father's chest (CPR was a thing of the future) and, getting no response, reached into my brother-in-law's black bag, took out a syringe, ripped open my father's shirt, and injected adrenaline into his heart. To no avail.

Later I was to lambaste myself for that unnecessary act. When reliving the scene I recalled enough of my neurological training to realize that the problem wasn't the heart: it was the brain. I had seen my father's eyes suddenly jerk to the right and should have known that no stimulant to the heart would have helped. He had had a massive cerebral hemorrhage (or thrombosis) on the right side. The eyes always look toward the site of the stroke.

At my father's funeral, I was not so cool headed. I've been told that when the time came for me to throw the first shovelful of dirt onto the coffin, I almost fainted and would have fallen into the open grave had not one of my relatives caught me.

My mother lived much longer, dying at ninety-three. I recall two memorable events at the time of her funeral.

The first involved baking. On the night before her funeral, I suddenly felt compelled to bake a batch of my mother's wonderful kichel. I suspect I needed distraction. Besides, baking kichel with my mother was a joyful memory, and I think I wanted a little more of her. I made the dough, let it rise overnight, and, early in the morning, rolled it out, added cinnamon, pineapple jam, and raisins, and baked it to serve to the family and friends returning to the house to sit with us after the funeral.

But the pastries were a failure! It's the only time that ever happened. I forgot to put in the sugar! Perhaps that was a symbolic message from me to myself that I had focused too much on my mother's dourness. It's as though my unconscious was nudging me: "You see, you've forgotten the good parts—her caring; her endless, often unspoken, devotion."

The second event was a powerful dream the night after the funeral. She's been dead now for fifteen years, but this dream image defies decay and still shines brilliantly in my mind's eye.

I hear my mother screeching my name. I hurry down the path to my childhood home, open the front door, and there, facing me, sitting on the stairway, row above row, are all the members of our extended family (all already dead—my mother, the last leaf, had outlived everyone in her community). As I look at those sweet faces on the stairs, I see my Aunt Minnie sitting in the very center. She is vibrating like a bumble bee, moving so quickly her features are blurred.

My Aunt Minnie had died a few months earlier. Her death had absolutely horrified me: a massive stroke paralyzed her, and, though conscious, she was unable to move a muscle in her body, aside from her eyelids. (This is known as the "locked-in" syndrome.) She remained like that until she died two months later.

But there she was in the dream—front and center and moving frenetically. I think it was a death-defying dream: there, on the stairs, no longer paralyzed, Minnie was moving again, and moving almost too quickly for the eye to see. In fact, the whole dream attempted to undo death. My mother was not dead; she was alive and calling me as she always did. And then I saw all the dead of my family, sitting on my stairs smiling, showing me that they were alive still.

I think, too, that there was another message, a "remember me" message. My mother called my name to tell me, "Remember me, remember all of us, don't let us perish." And so I have.

The phrase "Remember me" always moves me. In my novel *When Nietzsche Wept,* I portray Nietzsche wandering in a cemetery, eyeing the scattered tombstones, and composing a few lines of doggerel that end,

> *till stone is laid on stone*
> *and though none can hear*
> *and none can see*
> *each sobs softly: remember me, remember me.*

I wrote these lines for Nietzsche in a flash and was tickled at the opportunity of publishing my first bit of verse. Then, about a year later, I made a strange discovery. Stanford was moving the Department of Psychiatry to a new building, and during the move, my secretary found behind my file cabinet a large and bulging sealed manila envelope, yellowed with age, that had fallen out of sight long before. In the envelope was a lost packet of poetry I had written over several years during my adolescence and early adulthood. Among the verses were the identical lines, word for word, that I thought I had freshly composed for the novel. I had actually written them decades earlier, at the time of my fiancée's father's death. I had plagiarized myself!

While writing this chapter and thinking about my mother, I was visited by another disturbing dream.

A friend visits my home, and I show him around my garden and lead him into my study. I immediately see that my computer is missing, perhaps stolen. Not only that, but my large, usually heavily cluttered desk is entirely cleaned off.

It was a nightmare, and I awoke in panic. I kept saying to myself, "Calm down, calm down. What are you afraid of?" I knew, even during the dream, that my terror made no sense: after all, it was just a missing computer, and I had always had a complete backup of my computer elsewhere, in a safe place.

The next morning, while puzzling over the terror in my dream, I received a call from my sister, to whom I had sent a draft of the first part of this memoir. She was shaken by my memories, and described some of her own, including one I had forgotten. Our mother had been in the hospital following hip surgery, and my sister and I were at her apartment doing some of her paperwork when we received an urgent message from the hospital to come immediately. We rushed there and ran into her room, only to find a bare mattress: she had died, and her body had been removed. All evidence of her had vanished.

As I listened to my sister, the meaning of my dream crystallized. I understood the source of the terror in the dream: it was not the missing computer; it was that my desk, like my mother's bed, had been entirely cleaned off. The dream was of my death foretold.

PERSONAL ENCOUNTERS WITH DEATH

I experienced a close call when I was about fourteen. I had played in a chess tournament at the old Gordon Hotel on Seventeenth Street in Washington, D.C., and was waiting at the curbside for a bus home. While studying my notes of the chess game, a page slipped from my hand into the street, and I instinctively bent down to pick it up. A stranger jerked me back, and a taxi zoomed by at great speed, missing my head by inches. I was profoundly shaken by this incident and replayed the mental tape of it countless times. Even now, as I picture it, my heart speeds.

A few years ago, I experienced severe pain in my hip and consulted with an orthopedic surgeon, who ordered an x-ray. As we examined it together, he was foolish and insensitive enough to point to a small spot on the x-ray and comment in a matter-of-fact, doctor-to-doctor manner that it might be a metastatic lesion—in other words, a death sentence. He ordered an MRI that, because it was Friday, could not be done for three days. For those three agonizing days, death awareness took center stage in my mind. Of all the various ways I tried to find comfort, the most effective turned out to be—oddly enough—reading my own just-completed novel.

Julius, the protagonist of *The Schopenhauer Cure,* is an aging psychiatrist who is diagnosed with a fatal ma-lignant melanoma. I wrote many pages describing his struggle to come to terms with death and to live his remaining time in a meaningful manner. No ideas were able to help him until he opened Nietzsche's *Thus Spake Zarathustra* and considered the thought experiment of the eternal return. (See Chapter Four for how I use this idea in therapy.)

Julius ponders Nietzsche's challenge. Would he be willing to repeat his life as he had lived it, over and over again? He realizes that, yes, he has lived his life rightly, and . . . "after a few minutes Julius 'came to': he knew exactly what to do and how to spend his final year. He would live just the way he had lived the previous year—and the year before that and before that. He loved being a therapist, he loved connecting to others and helping to bring something to life in them . . . maybe he needed the applause, the affirmation and gratitude of those he helped. Even so, even if dark motives played their role, he was grateful for his work. God bless it!"

Reading my own words provided the comfort I had been seeking. *Consummate your life. Fulfill your potential.* Now I understood Nietzsche's counsel more fully. My own character, Julius, had shown me the way—a potent and unusual instance of life imitating fiction.

Fulfilling My Potential

I regard myself as an overachiever, having been a professor of psychiatry at Stanford University for decades and, in general, been treated with much respect by my colleagues and students. As a writer, I know I lack the poetic imagery of the great contemporary writers like Roth, Bellow, Ozick, McEwan, Banville, Mitchell, and countless others whose work I read with awe, but I have actualized what gifts I have. I'm a fairly good storyteller; have written both fiction and nonfiction; and have had far more readers and acclaim than I had ever dreamed possible.

Often in the past, contemplating an upcoming lecture, I imagined that some *éminence grise,* perhaps a senior training psychoanalyst, might stand up and declare that my comments were nothing but bullshit. But now that fear has evaporated: for one thing, I've gained confidence, for another, there is never anyone older than I in the audience.

For decades I have received much affirmation from readers and students. Sometimes I take it in and feel giddy. Sometimes, when I am entirely caught up in what I am writing that day, plaudits go only a millimeter deep. Sometimes I am astounded at others attributing to me far more wisdom than I possess, and I remind myself not to take such praise too seriously. Everyone needs to believe that there are truly wise men and women out there. I sought out such when younger, and now I, elderly and prominent, have become the suitable vessel for others' wishes.

I believe that our need for mentors reflects much about our vulnerability and wish for a superior or supreme being. Many people, including myself, not only cherish our mentors but often credit them with more than they deserve. A couple of years ago, at a memorial for a professor of psychiatry, I listened to a eulogy by one of my former students, whom I'll call

James, now an accomplished chairman of psychiatry at a university on the East Coast. I knew both men well, and it struck me that in his address, James was attributing a great many of his own creative ideas to his dead teacher.

Later that evening I mentioned my perception to James, who smiled sheepishly, said "Ah, Irv, still teaching me." He agreed that I was correct, but that he wasn't sure of his motivation. I am reminded of those ancient writers who attributed their own work to their teachers to such an extent that classical scholars today find it hard to determine the true authorship of many works. Thus for example, Thomas Aquinas attributed most of his own thoughts to his intellectual master, Aristotle.

When the Dalai Lama spoke at Stanford University in 2005, he was paid extraordinary reverence. His every utterance was idealized. At the end of his talk, a great many of my Stanford colleagues—eminent professors, deans, Nobel-level scientists—all rushed into line like schoolchildren to have him slip a prayer ribbon over their heads and to bow before him and call him "Your Holiness."

Each of us has a powerful desire to revere the great man or great woman, to utter the thrilling words "Your Holiness." Perhaps this is what Erich Fromm, in *Escape from Freedom,* meant by "lust for submission." It is the stuff from which religion emerges.

In sum, I feel that in my life and profession I have fulfilled myself and realized my potential. Such realization is not only satisfying; it is a buttress against transiency and impending death. Indeed, to a great extent my work as a therapist has always been part of my coping. I feel blessed to be a therapist: watching others open up to life is extraordinarily satisfying. Therapy offers opportunities *par excellence* for rippling. In every hour of work, I am able to pass along parts of myself, parts of what I have learned about life.

(As an aside, I often wonder how long this will continue to be true for our profession. In my practice, I've worked with several psychotherapists who, having just finished a graduate program consisting almost entirely of cognitive-behavioral therapy, feel despair at the prospect of working mechanically with patients in a behavioral prescriptive mode. And I wonder, too, where therapists trained to treat patients in this impersonal behavioral mode will turn when they themselves need help. Not to colleagues of their own school, I would wager.)

The idea of offering help to others with an intensive therapy approach focusing on interpersonal and existential issues and assuming the existence of an unconscious (though my view of the contents of the unconscious differs greatly from traditional analytic views) is precious to me, and the desire to keep it alive, to pass it along to others, provides meaning and encourages me to keep working and writing at my advanced age even though, as Bertrand Russell put it, "someday the solar system will lie in ruins." I can't quarrel with Russell's statement, yet I don't believe this cosmic view is relevant: it's only the human world, the world of human connections, that matters to me. I'd have no sadness, no grief at the thought of leaving an empty world, a world lacking another self-aware subjective mind. The idea of rippling, of passing along to others what has mattered to one life, implies connection with other self-aware essences; without that, rippling is impossible.

DEATH AND MY MENTORS

About thirty years ago, I began writing a textbook on existential psychotherapy. In preparation for that task, I worked for many years with patients facing imminent death from terminal illness. Many of them grew wise through their ordeal, served as my teachers, and had a lasting influence on my life and work.

Beyond these, I have had three outstanding mentors: Jerome Frank, John Whitehorn, and Rollo May. With each of these men I had a memorable encounter near the time of his death.

Jerome Frank

Jerome Frank was one of my professors at Johns Hopkins, a pioneer in group therapy and my guide into that field. Moreover, he has remained all my life a model of personal and intellectual integrity. After I finished my training, I stayed in close touch with him, visiting him regularly as he gradually declined in a Baltimore nursing home.

Jerry had progressive dementia in his nineties, and, on my last visit a few months before his death at the age of ninety-five, he did not recognize me. I stayed and spoke with him for a long time, recalling my memories of him and all the colleagues with whom he had worked. Gradually he remembered who I was and, shaking his head sadly, apologized for his memory loss.

"Very sorry, Irv, but it's beyond control. Every morning my memory, the whole slate, is wiped clean." He demonstrated this by swiping his hand across his forehead as if erasing a blackboard.

"That must be so awful for you, Jerry," I said. "I remember what pride you took in your extraordinary memory."

"You know, it's not that bad," he replied. "I wake up, have breakfast here on the ward with all these others patients and staff, who seem strangers every morning but later in the day grow more familiar. I watch TV and then I ask for someone to push my wheelchair over to the window, and I look out. I enjoy everything I see. A lot of things I see as if for the first time. I enjoy just seeing and looking. It's not so bad, Irv."

That was my last vision of Jerry Frank: in a wheelchair, neck bent over so far he had to strain to look up at me. He was suffering devastating dementia, yet was still reaching out to teach me that when one loses everything, there remains the pleasure of sheer being.

I treasure that gift, a final, end-of-life act of generosity by an extraordinary mentor.

John Whitehorn

John Whitehorn, a towering figure in psychiatry and the chairman of the Department of Psychiatry at Johns Hopkins for three decades, played a major role in my education. An awkward, courtly man, whose gleaming pate was fringed with a fastidiously clipped crescent of gray hair, he wore gold-rimmed spectacles and had not a wrinkle in his face or in the brown suit he wore every day of the year. (We students surmised that he must have had two or three identical ones in his closet.)

When Dr. Whitehorn lectured, he made no superfluous expressions: only his lips moved. All else—hands, cheeks, eyebrows—remained remarkably still. I never heard anyone, even his colleagues, call him by his first name. All the students dreaded his annual stilted cocktail party, where he served a tiny glass of sherry and not a bite of food.

During my third year of psychiatric residency, five senior residents and I spent every Thursday afternoon making rounds with Dr. Whitehorn. Beforehand, we were all served lunch in his oak-paneled office. The fare was simple, but served with Southern elegance: linen tablecloth, glistening silver trays, and bone china. The lunch conversation was long and leisurely. We each had calls to return and patients clamoring for our attention, but there was no way to rush Dr. Whitehorn. Ultimately even I, the most frenetic of the group, learned to slow down and put time on hold.

In these two hours we had the opportunity to ask him anything. I remember questioning him about such matters as the genesis of paranoia, a physician's responsibility to the suicidal, the incompatibility between therapeutic change and determinism. Although he always responded fully to such questions, he clearly preferred other subjects, such as the military strategy of Alexander the Great's generals, the accuracy of Persian archers, the major blunders of the battle of Gettysburg, and, most of all, his improved periodic table (he was originally trained as a chemist).

After lunch we sat in a circle observing Dr. Whitehorn interviewing the four or five patients on his service. It was never possible to predict the length of each interview. Some lasted fifteen minutes, others two or three hours. His pace was leisurely. He had plenty of time. Nothing interested him as much as a patient's

occupation and avocation. One week he would be prod-
ding a history professor to discuss in depth the failure
of the Spanish Armada, and the next week he would be
encouraging a South American planter to talk for an
hour about coffee trees—as though his paramount purpose was to understand the relationship between alti-
tude and the quality of the coffee bean. So subtly did he
shift into the personal domain that I was always startled
when a suspicious, paranoid patient suddenly began to
speak frankly about himself and his psychotic world.

By allowing a patient to teach him, Dr. Whitehorn
related to the *person,* rather than to the pathology, of
that patient. His strategy invariably enhanced both the
patient's self-regard and his or her willingness to be
self-revealing.

A "cunning" interviewer, one might say. Yet cunning he was not. There was no duplicity: Dr. Whitehorn genuinely wanted to be taught. He was a collector
of information and had in this manner over the years
accumulated an astounding trove of factual curios.

"You and your patients both win," he would say,
"if you let them teach you enough about their lives and
interests. You will not only be edified, but you will ultimately learn all you need to know about their illness."

He had a vast influence on my education—and on
my life. Many years later, I learned that his strong letter
of recommendation facilitated my being appointed to
the Stanford University faculty. After I began my

career at Stanford, I had no further contact with him for several years except for a few sessions with one of his cousins, whom he had referred to me for treatment.

And then, early one morning, I was stunned by a phone call from his daughter (whom I had never met) saying that he had suffered a massive stroke, was near death, and had specifically requested that I visit him. I immediately flew to Baltimore from California, all the while pondering the question, "Why me?" and went directly to his hospital bed.

He was hemiplegic, paralyzed on one side of his body, and had expressive aphasia, which greatly impaired his ability to speak.

How shocking to see one of the most gloriously articulate persons I had ever known drooling saliva and grubbing for words. He finally managing to utter, "I'm . . . I'm . . . I'm scared, damned scared." And I was scared, too, scared by the sight of a great statue felled and lying in ruins.

But why had he wanted to see *me*? He had trained two generations of psychiatrists, a great many of whom were in prominent positions at leading universities. Why choose me, an agitated, self-doubting son of a poor immigrant grocer? What could I possibly do for him?

I ended up not doing much. I behaved like any nervous visitor, searching desperately for some words of comfort until he fell asleep after twenty-five minutes. Later I learned that he died two days after my visit.

The question "Why me?" ran through my mind for years. Perhaps I was a stand-in for the son I knew he had lost in the horrendous World War II Battle of the Bulge.

I remember his retirement banquet, which happened to take place as I was completing my final year of training. At the end of the meal, after toasts and reminiscences by many dignitaries, he rose and began his farewell address in a stately fashion.

"I've heard it said," he began, "that one can judge a man by his friends. If that is true," here he paused to survey the audience with great deliberation, "then I must be a very fine fellow indeed." There have been times, not enough, that I have been able to apply this sentiment by saying to myself, "If he thought so well of me, then I must be a fine fellow indeed."

Much later, after I had gained distance and learned more about dying, I came to believe that Dr. Whitehorn died a lonely death—his was not a death surrounded by close and loving friends and family. That he reached out to me, a student whom he had not seen in ten years, and with whom he had never shared what I considered an intimate moment, indicates not so much any specialness on my part but rather his tragic lack of connectedness with people whom he cared for and who cared for him.

Looking back, I've often wished I'd had a second chance to visit him. I knew I had given him something simply by my willingness to fly across the country, but, oh, how I wish I could have done more. I should have touched him, taken his hand, perhaps even hugged him and kissed him on the cheek. But he was so stiff and so forbidding I doubt that anyone, for decades, had dared to hold him. I, for one, had never touched him nor seen anyone else do so. I wish I had told him how much he meant to me; how much his ideas had rippled into me; how often I thought of him when I spoke, in his manner, to patients. In some way, his request that I come to him as he lay dying was a mentor's final gift to me— though I'm certain that, in extremis as he was, nothing could have been further from his mind.

Rollo May

Rollo May mattered to me as an author, as a therapist, and, finally, as a friend.

During my early training in psychiatry, I felt confused and dissatisfied with the current theoretical models. It seemed to me that both the biological and the psychoanalytic models left out of their formulations too much of the human essence. When May's book *Existence* was published during my second year of residency, I devoured every page and felt that a bright, entirely new vista opened before me. I immediately embarked on an education in philosophy by enrolling in an undergraduate survey course in the history of Western philosophy. Ever since, I have continued reading and auditing courses in philosophy and found there more wisdom and guidance in my work than in the professional literature of my field.

I was grateful to Rollo May for that book and for pointing the way to a wiser approach to human problems. (I refer especially to his first three essays; the other essays were translations of European dasein-analysts, which I found less valuable.) Many years later when I developed death anxiety during my work with patients dying of cancer, I decided to enter therapy with him.

Rollo May lived and worked in Tiburon, an eighty-minute drive from my office at Stanford, but I felt it was worth the time, and saw him weekly for three years—except for three months each summer when he vacationed in New Hampshire. I tried to make constructive use of the commute time by taping our sessions and listening to the previous session during each trip—a technique I have since often suggested to my patients who have a long drive to my office.

We spoke a great deal about death and the anxiety that my work with so many dying patients had stirred up in me. It was the isolation accompanying death that most haunted me; and, at one point, when I was experiencing great nighttime anxiety during lecture trips, I arranged to spend the night at an isolated motel not far from his office and to have sessions with him before and after that night.

As predicted, I had a great deal of free-floating anxiety during the evening, with frightening dreams, including images of pursuit and a terrifying witch's hand coming through the window. Though we attempted to explore death anxiety, somehow I think we colluded in never staring at the sun: we avoided the full confrontation with the specter of death that I suggest in this book.

Overall, however, Rollo was an excellent therapist for me; and after we terminated, he reached out to me in friendship. He thought well of my *Existential Psychotherapy,* ten years in the writing, which I had just completed, and we negotiated with relative ease the complex and very tricky transition from a therapist-patient relationship to one of friendship.

As the years passed, there came a time when our roles changed. After Rollo suffered a series of small strokes, which frequently left him confused and panicky, he often turned to me for support.

One evening his wife, Georgia May, also a close friend, phoned to say that Rollo was near death and asked me and my wife to come immediately. That night the three of us remained together and took turns sitting with Rollo, who had lost consciousness and was breathing laboriously in advanced pulmonary edema. Ultimately, on my watch, he took one last convulsive breath and died. Georgia and I washed his body and prepared him for the mortician, who was to arrive in the morning to take him to the crematorium.

I went to bed that night very disturbed by Rollo's death and the thought of his cremation, and had this powerful dream:

I'm walking with my parents and sister in a mall and then we decide to go upstairs. I find myself on an elevator, but I'm alone—my family has disappeared. It's a long, long elevator ride. When I get off I'm on a tropical beach. But I can't find my family despite looking and looking for them. Although it is a lovely setting—tropical beaches are paradise for me—I begin to feel pervasive dread. Next I put on a nightshirt bearing a cute, smiling face of Smoky the Bear. That face on the shirt then becomes brighter, then brilliant. Soon the face becomes the entire focus of the dream, as though all the energy of the dream is transferred onto that cute grinning little Smoky the Bear face.

The dream woke me, not so much from terror, but from the brilliance of the blazing emblem on the nightshirt. It was as though floodlights were suddenly turned on in my bedroom. At the very beginning of the dream, I had felt calm, almost joyful, but as soon as I was unable to find my family, great foreboding and dread set in. After that, everything was taken over, the whole dream consumed, by that blazing Smoky the Bear.

I'm pretty sure that Rollo's cremation lay behind the blazing image of Smoky the Bear. Rollo's death confronted me with my own, which the dream portrays in my isolation from my family and by that endless elevator ride upstairs. I'm shocked by the gullibility of my unconscious. How embarrassing that some part of me has bought into the Hollywood version of immortality portrayed by that elevator ride and by the cinematic version of celestial paradise, replete with tropical beach. (Although paradise, because of its complete isolation, fell short of being entirely paradisiacal.)

The dream seems to represent some heroic efforts to diminish terror. I was shaken by the horror of Rollo's death and his pending cremation, and the dream struggled to defuse my terror by softening the entire experience. Death is disguised benignly as an elevator trip upstairs to a tropical beach. Even the fiery cremation is made into something more friendly and makes its appearance as a nightshirt, ready for the slumber of death, bearing an adorable image of the cuddly Smoky the Bear.

The dream seems a particularly felicitous example of Freud's belief that dreams are the guardians of sleep. My dream work strenuously attempted to keep me sleeping, to prevent my dream from turning into a nightmare. Like a dam, it held back the tide of terror, but ultimately cracked, allowing emotion to leak through. The adorable bear image eventually overheated and burst into a blaze so incandescent it jolted me awake.

My Personal Coping with Death

Few of my readers will fail to wonder whether, at seventy-five, I'm coping with my own death anxiety through the writing of this book. I need to be more transparent. I often ask patients the question, "What is it in particular that most frightens you about death?" I'll pose that question to myself.

The first thing that comes to me is the anguish of leaving my wife, my soul mate since we were both fifteen. An image enters my mind: I see her getting into her car and driving off alone. Let me explain. Every week I drive to see patients in San Francisco on Thursdays, and she takes the train Fridays to join me for the weekend. We then drive back together to Palo Alto, where I drop her off to retrieve her car at the train station parking lot. I always wait, watching through my rearview mirror to make certain she gets her car started, and only then do I drive away. The image of her getting into the car alone after my death, without my watching, without my protecting her, floods me with inexpressible pain.

Of course, you might say, that is pain about *her* pain. What about pain for myself? My answer is that there will be no "me" to feel pain. I am in accord with Epicurus's conclusion: "Where death is, I am not."

There won't be any me there to feel terror, sadness, grief, deprivation. My consciousness will be extinguished, the switch flicked off. Lights out. I also find comfort in Epicurus's symmetry argument: after death I will be in the same state of nonbeing as before birth.

Rippling

But I can't deny that writing this book about death is of value to me personally. I believe that it acts to desensitize me: I guess we can get used to anything, even death. Yet my primary purpose in writing this book is not to work through my own death anxiety. I believe I write primarily as a teacher. I've learned a great deal about tempering death anxiety and wish to transmit what I can to others while I'm still alive, still intellectually intact.

Thus the enterprise of writing is intimately associated with rippling. I find great satisfaction in passing something of myself into the future. But as I've said throughout this work, I don't expect that "I," my image, my persona, will persist, but rather that some idea of mine, something that provides guidance and comfort, will: that some virtuous, caring act or piece of wisdom or constructive way of dealing with terror will persist and spread out in wavelets in unpredictable ways among people I can never know.

Recently a young man consulted me about problems in his marriage and told me he had also come to satisfy his curiosity. Twenty years before, his mother (whom I could no longer recall) had seen me in therapy for a few sessions and had often spoken to him of me, telling him how her therapy with me had changed her life. Every therapist (and teacher) I know has similar stories of the long-term rippling effect.

I have let go of the wish, the hope, that I myself, my image, will persist in any tangible form. Certainly there will come a time when the last living person who has ever known me dies. Decades ago, I read in Alan Sharp's novel *A Green Tree in Gedde* a description of a country cemetery with two sections: the "remembered dead" and the "truly dead." The graves of the remembered dead are tended and adorned with flowers, whereas the graves of the truly dead were forgotten; they were flowerless, weed infested, with tombstones askew and eroded. These truly dead were the unknown ancient ones, the dead whom no one alive had ever seen. An old person—*every* old person—is the last repository of the image of many people. When the very old die, they each take a multitude with them.

Connections and Transiency

Intimate connections help me overcome the fear of death. I treasure my relationships with my family—my

wife, my four children, my grandchildren, my sister—
and with my network of close friends, many stretching
back for decades. I'm tenacious about maintaining and
nurturing old friendships; you cannot make new old
friends.

The rich opportunity for connection is precisely
what makes therapy so rewarding for the therapist. I
attempt to relate intimately and authentically with
every patient I see, in every hour we meet. A short time
ago, I commented to a close friend and colleague, also a
therapist, that even though I am seventy-five, the idea
of retirement remains distant from my mind.

"This work is so satisfying," I said, "I'd do it for
free. I consider it a privilege."

He responded instantly, "Sometimes I think I'd
pay to do it."

But are there no limits to the value of connections?
After all, you might ask, if we are born alone and must
die alone, then what lasting fundamental value can connection have? Whenever I consider that question, I
recall a comment a dying woman made in a therapy
group: "It's a pitch black night. I'm alone in my boat
floating in a harbor. I see the lights of many other boats.
I know I can't reach them, can't join with them. But
how comforting it is to see all those other lights bobbing
in the harbor."

I agree with her—rich connections temper the
pain of transiency. Many philosophers have expressed

other ideas to accomplish that goal. Schopenhauer and Bergson, for example, think of human beings as individual manifestations of an all-encompassing life force (the "Will," the "élan vital") into which a person is reabsorbed after death. Believers in reincarnation would claim that some essence of a human being—the spirit, soul, or divine spark—will persist and be reborn into another being. Materialists might say that after death, our DNA, our organic molecules, or even our carbon atoms are dispersed into the cosmos until called on to become part of some other life form.

For me these models of persistence do little to relieve the ache of transiency: the destiny of my molecules, sans my personal consciousness, provides me only cold comfort.

To me, transience is like background music: always playing, rarely noticed until some striking event brings it into full awareness. A recent incident in a group meeting comes to mind.

First some background on the meeting: I have been a member of a leaderless support group with ten other therapists for the past fifteen years, and for several months the group had centered on Jeff, a psychiatrist dying of an untreatable cancer. Ever since his diagnosis a few months before, Jeff had implicitly served as guide for all the other members on how to face death in a direct, thoughtful, and courageous manner. In the two prior meetings, Jeff had grown noticeably weaker.

In this meeting, I found myself immersed in a long reverie on transiency, which, immediately after the meeting, I tried to record in the following note. (Although we have a confidentiality rule, the group and Jeff gave me a special dispensation for this occasion.)

Jeff spoke of the days ahead when he will become too weak to meet with the group or to participate in it even if the group were to meet in his home. Was that the beginning of saying goodbye to us? Was he avoiding the pain of grief by withdrawing from us? He spoke of how our culture regards the dying as filth or trash, and how, consequently, we all withdraw from the dying.

"But has that happened here?" I asked.

He looked around at the group and shook his head. "No, not here. Here, it's different; you have, each of you, stayed with me."

Others spoke of needing to identify the boundary between caring for him and intruding—that is, are we asking too much from him? He is our teacher, he says. Teaching us to die. And he is right. I shall never forget him or his lessons. But his energy wanes.

Conventional therapy, he said, which had been useful in the past, is now no longer relevant. His wish is to talk about spiritual things—areas in which therapists do not tread.

"What do you mean by spiritual areas," we asked him.

After a long pause, he said, "Well, what is death? How do you go about dying? No therapist talks about that. If I am meditating upon my breathing and my breathing slows or stops, then what happens to my mind? What about afterward? Will there be some form of awareness even after the body, mere trash, is gone? No one can really say. Will it be okay to ask my family to allow my body to lie for three days (despite the leakage and odor)? Three days, in the Buddhist view, is the time needed for the spirit to clear the body. What about my ashes? Would the group like to distribute some of my ashes in a ceremony, perhaps in the midst of some ageless redwoods?"

Later, when he said he was more present, more completely and honestly present, with us in this group than anywhere else in his life, a rush of tears came to my eyes.

Suddenly—when another member talked about a nightmare of being buried in a casket while he was still conscious—a long-forgotten memory sprang into my mind. During my first year of medical school, I wrote a short story inspired by H. P. Lovecraft about that very theme: continued awareness in a buried man. I sent it to a sci-fi magazine, got a rejection notice, and put the story away somewhere (I've never found it) as I became consumed with studies. I forgot about it for 48 years until this moment in the group. But the memory taught me something about myself: I was dealing with anxiety about death much farther back than I had appreciated.

What an extraordinary meeting, I mused. In the history of humankind has any group ever held such a discussion? Nothing withheld. Nothing unspoken. The hardest, bleakest questions of the human condition stared at without blinking, without flinching.

I thought of a young woman patient I had seen earlier in the day who spent so much time bemoaning the crudity, the insensitivity of men. I looked around this all-male group. Each of these dear men had been so sensitive, so gentle, so caring, so extraordinarily present. Oh, how I wished she could have seen this group. How I wished the whole world could see this group!

And it was then that the thought of transience, lurking, whirring softly in the background, swept in. I realized with a thud that this unparalleled meeting was just as transient as our dying member. And as transient as all of us who trudged toward the death awaiting us just a bit farther down the road. And the fate of this perfect, this magnificent, this magisterial meeting? It will vanish. All of us, our bodies, our memory of this meeting, this note of my remembrances, Jeff's ordeal and his teaching, our offering such presence, everything will evaporate into thin air, leaving nothing except carbon atoms drifting in the darkness.

A wave of sadness swept over me. There must be a way to save it. If only this group had been filmed and then shown over some total earth channel watched by all living humans, it would change the world forever. Yes, that's the ticket— save, preserve, combat oblivion. Am I not addicted to preservation? Isn't that why I write books? Why am I writing this note? Isn't it some futile effort to record and preserve?

I thought of Dylan Thomas's line claiming that though lovers die, love survives. I was touched by it when I read it first, but now I wonder, "survive" where? As a pla-

tonic ideal? Are falling trees heard when there are no ears to hear?

Thoughts of rippling and connectivity ultimately filtered into my mind bearing a sense of relief and hope. Everyone in this group will be affected, perhaps forever, by what we had just witnessed today. Everyone is connected; everyone in this meeting will pass on to others, explicitly or implicitly, the lessons of life surfacing here. And the persons affected by the telling will in turn pass it to others. We cannot not communicate a lesson of such power. The ripples of wisdom, compassion, virtue will sweep on and on and on until . . . until . . . until . . .

A coda. Two weeks later, when we met in Jeff's home as he neared death, I again asked his permission to publish these notes and also whether he would prefer that I refer to him with a fictitious name or his real one. He asked that I use his real name, and I like to think that the idea of rippling, by virtue of this vignette, offered him a sliver of comfort.

RELIGION AND FAITH

I'm not a lapsed anything. As far as I can remember, I've never had any religious belief. I remember going to the synagogue on the high holidays with my father and reading the English translation of the services, which were an endless paean to the power and glory of God. I felt totally bewildered that the congregation paid homage to a deity so cruel, vain, vengeful, jealous, and thirsty for praise. I looked carefully at the bobbing heads and chanting faces of my adult relatives, hoping to see them grin at me. But they kept right on praying. I glanced at my Uncle Sam, always a jokester and a regular guy, and expected him to wink and whisper out of the side of his mouth, "Don't take this stuff too seriously, kiddo." But it never happened. He didn't wink or crack a smile: he looked straight ahead and kept right on chanting.

As an adult I attended a Catholic friend's funeral and listened to the priest proclaim that we would all meet again in heaven for a joyous reunion. Once again, I looked around at all the faces and saw nothing but fervent belief. I felt surrounded by delusion. Much of my skepticism may have been due to the crude pedagogical skills of my early religious teachers; perhaps if, at an early age, I had encountered a fine, sensitive, sophisticated teacher, I too would have been imprinted and unable to imagine a world without God.

In this book about fear of death, I have avoided writing extensively about religious consolation because of a cumbersome personal dilemma. On the one hand, because I believe that many of the ideas expressed in these pages will be of value even to readers with strong religious beliefs, I've avoided any phraseology that might prompt them to turn away. I respect persons of faith even if I do not share their views. On the other hand, my work is rooted in a secular, existential worldview that rejects supernatural beliefs. My approach assumes that life (including human life) has arisen from random events; that we are finite creatures; and that, however much we desire it, we can count on nothing besides ourselves to protect us, to evaluate our behavior, to offer a meaningful life schema. We have no predestined fate, and each of us must decide how to live as fully, happily, and meaningfully as possible.

However stark such a view may seem to some people, I do not find it so. If, as Aristotle holds, the premise that the faculty that makes us uniquely human is our rational mind, then we should perfect this faculty. Hence, orthodox religious views based on irrational ideas, such as miracles, have always perplexed me. I am personally incapable of believing in something that defies the laws of nature.

Try this thought experiment. Stare directly at the sun; take an unblinkered view at your place in existence; attempt to live without the protective railings many religions offer—that is, some form of continuation, immortality, or reincarnation, all of which deny death's finality. I think we can live well without the railings, and I agree with Thomas Hardy, who says that "if a way to the Better there be, it exacts a full look at the Worst."

I do not doubt that religious belief tempers the death fears of many. Yet to me it begs the question—it seems like an end run around death: death is not final, death is denied, death is de-deathified.

How do I work, then, with those of religious belief? Let me answer that in my preferred manner—by way of a story.

"Why Does God Send Me These Visions?": Tim

Some years ago I received a call from Tim, who asked for a one-time consultation to help him deal with, as he put it, "the most important question in existence—or my existence." Then he added, "Let me repeat, only a single consultation. I'm a religious man."

A week later he entered my office, in white paint-stained Dutch artist overalls, carrying a portfolio of drawings. He was a short, rotund, large-eared man, with a graying crew cut and a huge smile displaying teeth resembling a white picket fence with several pickets kicked out. He wore glasses so thick I was reminded of the bottom of Coca-Cola bottles. He held a small tape recorder and asked to record our session.

I agreed and obtained preliminary basic information. He was sixty-five, divorced; he had built homes for the past twenty years and had retired four years ago to concentrate on his art. And then, with no prompting from me, he jumped right in.

"I called you because I once read your book *Existential Psychotherapy,* and you sounded like a wise man."

"And how come," I asked, "you want to see this wise man only once?"

"Because I have only one question, which I trust you are wise enough to answer in a single session."

Surprised at his lightning-quick reply, I looked at him. He averted his gaze, looked out the window, fidgeted, and then stood up and sat down twice and clutched his portfolio more tightly.

"Is that the only reason?"

"I knew you were going to ask that. I often know in advance exactly what people are going to say. But back to your question of why only a single visit. I gave you the important answer, but there are others. Three to be exact. One—finances are satisfactory but not excellent. Two—your book is wise, but it's clear you're an unbeliever, and I'm not here to defend my faith. Three—you're a shrink, and every shrink I've met has tried to put me on pills."

"I like your clarity and the way you speak your mind, Tim. I try to do the same. I'll do my best to help in our one meeting. What is your question?"

"I've been a lot of things besides a builder." Tim spoke quickly, as though he had rehearsed this. "I've been a poet. A musician when I was young—I performed on the piano and the harp and have composed some classical music and one opera that has been performed

by a local amateur group. But for the last three years
I've been painting, nothing but painting. This here," he
nodded toward the portfolio, still clutched under his
arm, "is the work of just the last month."

"And the question?"

"All my paintings and drawings are simply copies
of visions that God has sent to me. Almost nightly now,
just between sleep and waking, I get a vision from God,
and I spend the entire next day, or days, just copying
down the vision. My question to you is, *why does God
send me these visions?* Look."

He opened his portfolio carefully, obviously hesi-
tant about my seeing all the work, and pulled out a
large drawing. "Here's an example from last week."

It was a remarkable pen-and-ink drawing done
with meticulous detail of a nude man lying face down
on the earth hugging the ground, possibly even copu-
lating with the earth, while the surrounding bushes
and branches of trees bent toward him and appeared
to be tenderly stroking him. A number of animals—
giraffes, skunks, camels, tigers—encircled him, each
with head bent as though paying homage. On the
lower margin he had scrawled, "Loving mother
earth."

He began rapidly pulling out one drawing after
another. I was dazzled by his bizarre, twisted, arresting
drawings and acrylics teeming with archetypal symbols,
Christian iconography, and several mandalas with blazing colors.

I had to tear myself away as I noted the clock: "Tim, our hour is running out, and I want to try to answer your question. I have two observations about you. My first observation is that you are extraordinarily creative and have shown evidence of this all through your life—your music, your opera, your poetry, and now your extraordinary artwork. My second observation is that your self-esteem is very low: I don't believe you recognize and appreciate your gifts. You with me so far?"

"I guess so," said Tim, looking embarrassed and then, without looking at me, added, "Not the first time I heard this."

"So my view of what's happening is that these ideas and these remarkable drawings emerge from your own creative wellspring, but that your self-regard is so low, you're so self-doubting, that you cannot believe that you are capable of such creations, so you automatically pass the credit to someone else, in this case to God. So my point is that, even though *your creativity may be God-given*, I'm convinced that you, and you alone, created the visions and the drawings."

Tim nodded while listening carefully. He pointed to the tape recorder and said, "I want to remember this, and I'll listen a lot to this tape. I think you've given me what I've needed."

When I work with someone who is religious, I follow the precept that stands alone at the top of my personal hierarchy of values: *caring for my patient.* There is nothing I allow to interfere with that. I cannot imagine attempting to undermine any belief system that is serving a person well, even a belief system that appears entirely fantastical to me. Thus, when persons with religious faith seek my help, I never challenge their core belief, often one that has been engrained since early life. On the contrary, I often search for ways to support their belief.

I worked with a priest once who had always taken great comfort in his early morning pre-Mass conversation with Jesus. At the time I saw him, he was so harried by administrative tasks and by a conflict with peers in his diocese that he had taken to cutting these conversations short or skipping them entirely. I set about exploring why he had deprived himself of something that gave him so much comfort and guidance. Together we worked through his resistance. It never occurred to me to question his practice or in any way instill doubt.

I do, however, recall one glaring exception, an episode in which I lost some of my therapeutic bearings.

How Can You Live Without Meaning?:
The Orthodox Rabbi

Years ago, a young orthodox rabbi visiting from abroad phoned to request a consultation. He said he was training to become an existential therapist but was experiencing some dissonance between his religious background and my psychological formulations. I agreed to see him, and a week later he bounded into my office, an attractive young man with piercing eyes, a long beard, peyos (long curly sideburns), a yarmulke, and, oddly, tennis shoes. For thirty minutes, we spoke in generalities about his desire to become a therapist and the conflicts between his religious beliefs and many specific statements in my textbook *Existential Psychotherapy*.

At first deferential, his demeanor slowly changed, and he began to voice his beliefs with such zeal as to make me suspect that the real purpose of his visit was to convert me to the religious life. (It would not be the first time that I had been visited by a missionary.) As his voice rose and his words increased in tempo, I regrettably grew impatient and far more blunt and incautious than is my wont.

"Your concern is a real one, Rabbi," I interjected. "There *is* a fundamental antagonism between our views. Your belief in an omnipresent, omniscient personal God watching you, protecting you, providing you with a life design, is incompatible with the core of my existential vision of humanity as free, mortal, thrown alone and randomly into an uncaring universe. In your view," I continued, "death is not final. You tell me that death is merely a night between two days and that the soul is immortal. So, yes, there is *indeed* a problem in your wish to become an existential therapist: our two points of view are diametrically opposed."

"But you," he responded with intense concern on his face, "how can you live with only these beliefs? And without meaning?" He shook his forefinger at me. "Think hard. How can you live without belief in something greater than yourself? I tell you it's not possible. It's living in the dark. Like an animal. What meaning would there be if everything is destined to fade? My religion provides me with meaning, wisdom, morality, with divine comfort, with a way to live."

"I don't consider that a rational response, Rabbi. Those commodities—meaning, wisdom, morality, living well—are *not* dependent on a belief in God. And, yes, *of course,* religious belief makes you feel good, comforted, virtuous—that is exactly what religions are invented to do. You ask how I can live. I believe I live well. I'm guided by human-generated doctrines. I believe in the Hippocratic oath I took as a physician, and dedicate myself to helping others heal and grow. I live a moral life. I feel compassion for those about me. I live in a loving relationship with my family and friends. I don't need religion to supply a moral compass."

"How can you say that?" he interjected. "I have great sorrow for you. There are times I feel that, without my God, my daily rituals, my beliefs, I'm not sure I could live."

"And there are times," I replied, entirely losing my patience, "when I think that if I had to devote my life to belief in the unbelievable and spend my day following a regimen of 613 daily rules and glorifying a God who dotes on human praise, I'd consider hanging myself!"

At this point the rabbi reached for his yarmulke. *Oh-oh,* I thought; *oh no, he's not going to chuck it away. I went too far! Much too far! I impulsively said more than I intended.* Never, never has it been my desire to undermine anyone's religious faith.

But no, he was simply reaching up to scratch his head and to express baffled wonder at the wide ideological gulf separating us and that I had drifted so far from my heritage and cultural background. We ended our session amiably and parted, he heading north, I heading south. I never learned whether he continued his study of existential psychotherapy.

ON WRITING A BOOK ABOUT DEATH

A final word on writing about death. It is natural for a self-reflective seventy-five-year-old to wonder about death and transiency. The everyday data are too powerful to ignore: my generation is passing, my friends and colleagues grow ill and die, my vision fades, and I receive ever more frequent distress signals from various somatic outposts—knees, shoulders, back, neck.

In my youth, I heard my parents' friends and relatives say that all the Yalom men were gentle—and that

they all died young. I believed in that early death scenario for a long time. Yet here I am at seventy-five. I've
outlived my father by many years, and I know I live on
borrowed time.

Isn't the creative act in itself entwined with concern about finiteness? Such was the belief of Rollo May,
a fine writer and painter, whose lovely cubistic painting
of Mount St. Michel hangs in my office. Persuaded that
the act of creation permits us to transcend our fear of
death, he continued writing almost to the very end.
Faulkner expressed the same belief: "The aim of every
artist is to arrest motion, which is life, by artificial
means and hold it fixed so that a hundred years later,
when a stranger looks at it, it moves again." And Paul
Theroux said that death was so painful to contemplate
that it causes us to "to love life and value it with such
passion that it may be the ultimate cause of all joy and
all art."

The act of writing itself feels like renewal. I love
the act of creation from the first glimmering of an idea
to the final manuscript. I find the sheer mechanics to be
a source of pleasure. I love the carpentry of the writing
process: finding the perfect word, sanding and burnish-
ing rough sentences, tinkering with the tick-tocks of
phrase and sentence cadence.

Some think that my immersion in death must be
deadening. When I lecture on the subject, often a colleague will respond that I must be living a grim life to

dwell so much on such dark issues. If you believe that, I say to them, then I haven't done my job. I try again to convey that facing death dispels grimness.

Sometime I can best describe my inner state by using the metaphor of the "split screen" technique. This hypnotic therapy technique helps patients detoxify some haunting painful memory. Here's the procedure: the therapist asks hypnotized patients to close their eyes and split their visual horizon, or screen, into two horizontal parts: on half the screen, the patient places the dark or traumatic image; on the other half, a lovely scene, one providing pleasure and tranquility (for example, a stroll on a favorite forest trail or tropical beach). The continued presence of the tranquil scene offsets and tempers the disturbing image.

One half of my conscious screen is sober and always aware of transience. The other half, however, offsets it by playing a different show, a scenario I can best describe by a metaphor suggested by the evolutionary biologist Richard Dawkins, who asks us to imagine a laser-thin spotlight moving inexorably along the immense ruler of time. Everything that the beam has passed is lost in the darkness of the past; everything ahead of the spotlight is hidden in the darkness of the yet to be born. Only what is lit by the laser-thin spotlight lives. This image dispels grimness and evokes in me the thought of how staggeringly lucky I am to be here, alive, and luxuriating in the pleasure of sheer being! And how tragically foolish it would be to diminish my brief time in the life-light by adopting life-negating schemes which proclaim that real life is to be found elsewhere in the utterly indifferent immense darkness ahead of me.

Writing this book has been a journey, a poignant journey backward, back to my childhood and my parents. Events from long ago pull at me. I've been astonished to see that death has shadowed me my entire life, and astonished too by the persistence and clarity of so many memories associated with death. The capriciousness of memory, too, strikes me with much force—for example, that my sister and I, once living in the same household, recall such different events.

As I age, I find the past ever more with me—as Dickens describes so beautifully in the epigraph that opens this chapter. Perhaps I am doing as he suggests: completing the circle, smoothing out rough spots of my story, embracing all that has made me and all that I have become. When I revisit childhood sites and attend school reunions, I am more moved than I used to be. Perhaps I feel joy in finding that there is yet a "there" there, that the past doesn't truly vanish, that I can revisit it at will. If, as Kundera says, death's terror stems from the idea of the past vanishing, then reexperiencing the past is vital reassurance. Transiency is stayed—if only for a while.

Chapter 7

ADDRESSING DEATH ANXIETY

Advice for Therapists

I am human, and nothing human is alien to me.
TERENCE

Although this final chapter is addressed to therapists, I have attempted to write in a jargon-free
manner, and it is my hope that any reader can understand and appreciate these words. So even if you are not
a therapist, please keep reading.

My approach to psychotherapy is not mainstream.
Few therapy training programs emphasize (or even
mention) an existential approach in their curriculum;
consequently, many therapists may find my comments
and my clinical vignettes odd. To explain my approach,

I first need to clarify the term *existential,* about which much confusion swirls.

WHAT DOES EXISTENTIAL MEAN?

For many philosophically informed individuals, the term *existential* evokes a pastiche of meanings: Kierkegaard's Christian existentialism emphasizing freedom and choice; Nietzsche's iconoclastic determinism; Heidegger's focus on temporality and authenticity; Camus' sense of absurdity; Jean Paul Sartre's stress on commitment in the face of absolute gratuitousness.

In clinical work, however, I use the word "existential" in a straightforward manner simply to refer to existence. Although existential thinkers emphasize different perspectives, they share the same basic premise: *we humans are the only creatures for whom our own existence is the problem.* So *existence* is my key concept. I could just as well use such terms as "existence therapy" or "existence-focused therapy." It is only because these seemed cumbersome that I use the sleeker term "existential psychotherapy."

The existential approach is one of many psychotherapy approaches, all with the same raison d'être—to minister to human despair. The existential therapeutic position states that what bedevils us issues *not only* from our biological genetic substrate (a psychopharmacological model), *not only* from our struggle with repressed instinctual strivings (a Freudian position), *not only* from our internalized significant adults who may be uncaring, unloving, or neurotic (an object relations position), *not only* from disordered forms of thinking (a cognitive-behavioral position), *not only* from shards of forgotten traumatic memories or from current life crises involving one's career and relationship with significant others, *but also—but also*—from a confrontation with our existence.

The bedrock position of existential therapy posits, then, that in addition to other sources of despair, we suffer also from our inevitable confrontation with the human condition—the "givens" of existence.

What precisely are these "givens"?

The answer is within each of us and readily available. Set aside some time and meditate on your own existence. Screen out diversions, bracket all preexisting theories and beliefs, and reflect on your "situation" in the world. In time you will inevitably arrive at the deep structures of existence or, to use the theologian Paul Tillich's felicitous term, *ultimate concerns*. In my view, four ultimate concerns are particularly germane to the practice of therapy: death, isolation, meaning in life, and freedom. These four ultimate concerns constitute the spine of my 1980 textbook, *Existential Psychotherapy,* in which I discuss, in detail, the phenomenology and the therapeutic implications of each of these concerns.

Though in everyday clinical work the four are intertwined, the fear of death is the most prominent and bedeviling ultimate concern. As therapy progresses, however, concerns about meaning in life, isolation, and freedom emerge as well. Existentially oriented therapists with a different perspective may report a different hierarchy: Carl Jung and Viktor Frankl, for example, emphasize the high incidence of patients who seek therapy because they have lost any sense of meaning in life.

The existential worldview on which I base my clinical work embraces rationality, eschews supernatural beliefs, and posits that life in general, and our human life in particular, has arisen from random events; that, though we crave to persist in our being, we are finite creatures; that we are thrown alone into existence without a predestined life structure and destiny; that each of us must decide how to live as fully, happily, ethically, and meaningfully as possible.

Does existential therapy exist? Though I speak repeatedly and familiarly of existential psychotherapy (and have written a lengthy textbook by that title), I have never considered it a freestanding ideological school. Rather, it is my belief and my hope that a well-trained therapist who has knowledge of, and skills from, many therapeutic approaches *should also be trained to have a sensibility for existential issues.*

Although my intention in this chapter is to increase the sensibility of therapists to vital existential issues and to encourage their willingness to address them, I believe that this sensibility is rarely sufficient for an overall positive outcome: in almost every course of treatment, therapeutic skills from other orientations will need to come into play.

DISTINGUISHING CONTENT AND PROCESS

At times when I lecture about the necessity of considering the human condition in therapy, a student therapist may (and should) respond, "These ideas about our place in existence have the ring of truth to them, but they seem so airy, so insubstantial. What does an existential therapist actually *do* in the therapy hour?" Or a student may ask, "If I were a fly on the wall in your office, what would I see happen during your therapy hours?"

I respond by first offering a tip about how to observe and comprehend psychotherapy sessions—a tip that all therapists learn early in their training and that will continue to prove valuable after many decades of practice. The tip is deceptively simple: *distinguish between content and process.* (In this context I use "process" to refer to the nature of the therapy relationship.)

The meaning of *content* is obvious: it refers simply to the topics and issues discussed. There will be times when the patient and I spend much time discussing the ideas expressed in this book but often for weeks on end there will be no existential content as a patient discusses other concerns related to such issues as relationships, love, sex, career choices, parenting problems, or money.

In other words, existential content may be salient for some (but not all) clients at some (but not all) stages of their therapy. That is as it should be. The effective therapist should never try to force some area of content: therapy should not be theory-driven but relationship-driven.

It is a far different matter when you examine a session not for content but for "relationship" (often referred to in the professional literature as "process"). The therapist who has a sensibility to existential issues relates differently to a patient than one who does not—*a difference that is evident in every single session.*

Thus far in this book, I have said much about existential content; most of the vignettes I have described focus on the mutative power of ideas (for example, Epicurean principles, rippling, fulfilling oneself). But generally ideas are not enough: *it is the synergy of "ideas-plus-relationship" that creates real therapeutic power.* In this chapter, I will offer a number of suggestions to help you, the therapist, increase the meaningfulness and effectiveness of the therapy relationship, which will in turn enhance your ability to help your patients confront and overcome the terror of death.

The idea that the texture of the relationship is crucial to therapeutic change is nothing new. For a century, psychotherapy clinicians and teachers have realized that it is not primarily theory or ideas, but the *relationship* that heals. Early analysts knew it was essential to have a solid therapeutic alliance and, consequently, scrutinized in minute detail the interaction between therapist and patient.

If we accept the premise (and its persuasive body of supporting research) that the therapeutic relationship is instrumental in psychotherapy, the next obvious question is, What type of relationship is most effective? Over sixty years ago, Carl Rogers, a pioneer in psychotherapy research, demonstrated that improvement in therapy was associated with a triad of therapist behaviors: genuineness, accurate empathy, and unconditional positive regard.

These therapist characteristics are important in all forms of therapy, and I endorse them strongly. I believe, however, that in working with death anxiety or any existential issue, the concept of genuineness takes on a different, far-reaching meaning that results in radical changes in the nature of the therapeutic relationship.

THE POWER OF CONNECTION IN OVERCOMING DEATH ANXIETY

When I keep my gaze fixed on the existential facts of life, I perceive no clear boundary between my patients, the afflicted, and myself, the healer. Ordinary role descriptions and characterological diagnoses impede, rather than facilitate, therapy. Because I believe that the antidote to much anguish is sheer connectedness, I try to live in the hour with my patient without erecting artificial and unnecessary barriers. In the process of therapy, I am an expert but not infallible guide to my patient. I've taken this journey before—in my own voyage of exploration and as a guide to many others.

In my work with clients, I strive for connectedness above all else. To that end, I am resolved to act in good faith: no uniforms or costumes; no parading of diplomas, professional degrees, and awards; no pretense of knowledge I do not possess; no denying that existential dilemmas strike home for me as well; no refusal to answer questions; no hiding behind my role; and, finally, no concealing my own humanness and my own vulnerabilities.

Wild Dogs Barking in the Cellar: Mark

I'll begin by describing a therapy session that illustrates several aspects of the influence of an existential sensibility on the therapeutic relationship, including a greater focus on the here-and-now and greater therapist self-disclosure. This session occurred in the second year of therapy with Mark, a forty-year-old psychotherapist who first sought therapy because of persistent death anxiety and unresolved grief for his sister. (Mark is briefly discussed in Chapter Three.)

In the few months prior to this session, his preoccupation with death had been replaced by a new issue: a sexual infatuation with one of his patients, Ruth.

I began the session in an unusual way by telling Mark that I had that morning referred a thirty-year-old man to him for group therapy. "If he contacts you," I said, "please phone, and I'll give you further information about our conversation."

At Mark's nod, I went on, "So, where shall we start today?"

"Same old stuff. As usual, on my drive over here, I thought about Ruth big-time. Hard to get her out of my mind. Last night I went out to dinner with some of my old high school chums, and they were all reminiscing about our dating experiences back then, and I got to obsessing about Ruth again—just started aching for her."

"Can you describe your obsessing? Tell me exactly what goes on in your mind."

"Oh, that stupid, childish, starry-eyed feeling. I feel so dumb—I'm all grown up. I'm forty years old. I'm a psychologist. She's my patient, and I know there'll be no follow-up."

"Stay with the starry-eyed feeling," I said. "Sink into it. Tell me what comes to you."

He closed his eyes. "Lightness, feels like I am flying . . . no thoughts of my poor dead sister . . . no thoughts of death . . . suddenly I'm flashing on a scene: I'm sitting on my mother's lap, and she's hugging me. I must be about age five or six—it was before she got cancer."

"So," I ventured, "when the starry-eyed feeling settles in, death disappears and, along with it, all thoughts about your sister's death, and you're once again a young boy being held by your mother before she developed cancer."

"Well, yes, I never thought of it quite that way."

"Mark, I wonder if the bliss of the starry-eyed feeling doesn't relate to merger, the sense of the lonely 'I' dissolving into the 'we.' And it seems to me that the other major player here is sex—the force that is so vital it can, at least temporarily, push death off the stage of your mind. So, I'm thinking that your infatuation with Ruth combats your death anxiety in two potent ways. No wonder you hang on to your infatuation so tenaciously."

"You're right on when you say sex 'temporarily' pushes death out of my mind. I had a pretty good week, but thoughts of death kept coming back, kept intruding. On Sunday I took my daughter on a motorcycle ride to La Honda and then on down to the ocean at Santa Cruz—it was a glorious day, but the thought of death kept hounding me. 'How many more times you gonna be able to do this?' I kept asking myself. Everything passes—I'm getting older, daughter getting older."

"These thoughts of death," I said, "let's keep analyzing them; let's dissect them. I know that the thought of death feels overwhelming—but stare right into it, tell me, what in particular is the most frightening thing about dying?"

"The pain of dying, I guess. My mother had a lot of pain—but, no, that's not the main thing. Mostly it's the fear of how my daughter will cope. Almost always the tears start to flow when I think of how she'll be when I die."

"Mark, I believe you were overexposed to death—too much, too soon. You had a mother who developed cancer when you were a child, and you watched her dying for the next ten years. And without a father. But your daughter has had a different and healthy mother and a father who takes her on beautiful Sunday motorcycle rides to the ocean and is present in every way. I think you're putting your own experience into her—I mean you're projecting your fears and your mind-set onto her."

Mark nodded, was silent for a while, then turned to me, "Let me ask you something: how do *you* deal with it? Doesn't the fear of death get to you?"

"I have my three A.M. bouts with anxiety about dying, too, but they occur far less now, and, as I grow older, gazing at death has some positive results: I feel more poignancy, more vitality, in my life; death makes me live more in each moment—valuing and appreciating the sheer pleasure of awareness, of being alive."

"But what about your kids? Don't you worry about their response to your death?"

"I don't worry much about that. I feel the parents' job is to help their kids become autonomous, to grow away from them, and to become going concerns. My kids are okay in that department—they'll grieve, but they'll get on with life. Just as your daughter will."

"You're right. With my rational mind, I know she'll do all right. In fact, I've had a notion recently that maybe I could set a model for her about how to face death."

"What a wonderful idea, Mark. What a wonderful gift to your daughter."

After a brief pause, I went on, "Let me ask you something about the here-and-now, about you and me today. This session has been different—more than other sessions, you've asked *me* a lot of questions. And I've tried to answer them. How has that felt?"

"It's good. Very good. Every time you share yourself with me like that, I begin to realize I need to be more open in my own therapy practice."

"There's another thing I want to ask about. At the very beginning of the session, you said that 'as usual' you began thinking about Ruth on the way to see me. What do you make of that? Why on the way to see me?"

Mark fell silent, slowly shaking his head.

"Is it perhaps relief from the difficult work you imagine having to face here?" I ventured.

"No, that's not it. Here's what it is." Mark paused, as if screwing up his courage. "It's to distract me from another question. Here's the question: How do you feel about me, how do you judge me as a therapist for the whole Ruth episode?"

"I can empathize with you, Mark. I've been sexually aroused by patients, and so has every other therapist I know. Now, there's no doubt that you, as you yourself put it, went over the top and got too consumed, but sex has a way of defeating reason. I know that your integrity is such that you will not act on your infatuation with your patient. And I think that perhaps in an odd way our work has encouraged your going so far in your feelings. I mean that you took constraints off yourself because you knew you had me here every week as a safety net."

"But don't you judge me as incompetent?"

"What do you make of my sending you a patient today?"

"Yeah, right—I've got to let that sink in. That's a very strong message, I know—and I feel so affirmed by you doing that I can hardly find the words to express it.

"And yet," Mark continued, "there's still some small voice in my head saying that you must think I'm a shit."

"No, I don't. It's time to press the delete button on that thought. We're out of time today, but there's something else I want to say to you: this journey you've been on, this experience with Ruth, is not all bad. I truly believe that you're going to learn and grow from what's happened. Let me adapt some of Nietzsche's words and say this to you: 'To become wise you must learn to listen to the wild dogs barking in your cellar.'"

That hit home—Mark whispered the words to himself. He left the office with tears in his eyes.

Along with issues of connection, this session illustrates a number of other existential themes that I'll now discuss in turn: love bliss, sex and death, dissecting the fear of death, the therapeutic act and the therapeutic word, using the here-and-now in therapy, and Terence's maxim and therapist self-disclosure.

LOVE BLISS The mechanism Mark described at the beginning of the session—his "starry-eyed" feeling and the unbounded joy radiating from his infatuation, along with his memory of similar bliss when he was cradled in his mother's lap in the good times, before her cancer had started to do its work—is often present in love infatuations. In the mind of an obsessed lover, other concerns are pushed off stage: the beloved—her every word, her every mannerism, even her foibles— claims all of his attention. Thus, when Mark was snug in his mother's lap, the pain of his isolation evaporated because he was no longer a lonely "I." My comment, "The lonely 'I' dissolves into the 'we'"—clarified the way his obsession had assuaged that pain. I don't know whether that phrase is original with me or whether I read it eons ago, but I have found it useful with many love-bewitched patients.

SEX AND DEATH In respect to the issue of sex and death, not only did love-merger assuage Mark's existential anxiety, but another death-anxiety emollient—the power of sexuality—kicked in. Sex, the vital life force, often counters thoughts of death. I've encountered many instances of this mechanism: the patient with a severe coronary who was so sexually driven that in an ambulance carrying him to the emergency room, he attempted to grope an ambulance attendant; or the widow who felt overcome with sexual feelings while driving to her husband's funeral; or the elderly widower, terrified by death, who became uncharacteristically sexually driven and had so many sexual affairs with women in his retirement community and created such divisiveness that the management demanded he seek psychiatric consultation. Still another elderly woman, after her twin sister had died from a stroke, became so overcome with multiple orgasms while using a vibrator that she feared she too would suffer a stroke. Worried lest her daughters discover the vibrator next to her body, she decided to dispose of it.

DISSECTING THE FEAR OF DEATH To address Mark's fear of death, I asked him—as I asked other patients in earlier vignettes—to tell me what in particular frightened him most about dying. Mark's answer was different from those of others who said, "All the things I would not have done," "I want to see the ends of stories," "No more me." Instead, he was anxious about how his daughter would cope without him. I addressed this fear by helping him see its irrationality and that he was projecting his own issues onto his daughter (who had a fully present, loving mother and father). I strongly supported his resolution to offer his daughter a gift—a model of how one may face death with equanimity. (In

Chapter Five I discussed a group in which several terminally ill patients made a similar resolution.)

THE THERAPEUTIC ACT AND THE THERAPEUTIC WORD I began the therapy hour by announcing that I had referred a patient to Mark for group therapy. Almost all teachers of psychotherapy are highly critical of establishing such a dual relationship—that is, any type of secondary relationship with a psychotherapy patient. Referring a patient to Mark had its potential hazards: for example, his eagerness to please me might have made it difficult for him to be truly present with that patient; it might have resulted in there being three persons in the relationship—Mark, the patient, and my hovering ghost influencing Mark's words and feelings.

Dual relationships are, indeed, generally not in the best interests of the therapy process, but in this instance I regarded the risk as low and the potential payoff high. Before Mark became my patient, I had supervised his group therapy work and considered him a competent group therapist. Moreover, he had consistently done excellent work with referrals in the past few years before he started therapy with me.

When, at the very end of the session, he voiced self-derogatory beliefs and persisted in believing that I too had a low opinion of him, I had an exceedingly powerful response: *I reminded him that I had just referred a patient to him.* This act was infinitely more supportive than any words of reassurance I might have uttered. The therapeutic act is far more effective than the therapeutic word.

UsING THE HERE-AND-Now IN THERAPY Note the two instances during the session when I shifted into the here-and-now. Mark began the hour by saying that "as usual" on the way to my office he had slipped into an enchanting reverie about his patient, Ruth. That comment obviously had implications for our relationship. I stored it and, later in the session, inquired about why, on the way to see me, he habitually obsesses about Ruth.

Later Mark posed several questions to me about my death anxiety and about my children, and I responded to each question, but made sure of taking the next step of exploring his feelings about posing questions to me and about my answering them. *Therapy is always an alternating sequence of interaction and reflection upon that interaction.* (I'll have more to say about this idea when I discuss the here-and-now later in this chapter.) Finally, the session with Mark illustrates the synergy between ideas and relationship: both factors were at work in this session, as in most therapy sessions.

TERENCE's MAXIM AND THERAPIST SELF-DISCLOSURE Terence, a second-century Roman playwright, offers an aphorism that is extraordinarily important in the inner work of the therapist: *I am human, and nothing human is alien to me.*

Thus, at the end of the session when Mark gathered the courage to ask a question he had long suppressed—"How do you judge me as a therapist for the whole Ruth episode?"—I chose to answer that I could empathize with him because I've also at times been sexually aroused by patients. I added that this was also true of every therapist I've ever known.

Mark posed an uncomfortable question, but, when faced with it, I followed Terence's maxim and searched my own mind for some similar recollection and then shared it. No matter how brutal, cruel, forbidden, or alien a patient's experience, you can locate in yourself some affinity to it if you are willing to enter into your own darkness.

Beginning therapists would do well to use Terence's axiom as a mantra, helping them empathize with their patients by locating their own similar internal experiences. This aphorism is particularly apt in work with patients with death anxiety. If you are to be truly present with such patients, you must open yourself to your own death anxiety. I don't mean to be glib about this: it is no easy task, and no training program prepares therapists for this type of work.

FOLLOW-UP Over the following ten years, I met with Mark twice for brief therapy for recurrences of death anxiety, once when a close friend died and once when he himself required surgery for a benign tumor. Each time he responded quickly to a few sessions. Eventually he felt strong enough to see several patients in his own practice who were encountering death anxiety as they underwent chemotherapy.

Timing and the Awakening Experience: Patrick

Up to now, I have for pedagogical reasons discussed ideas and relationship separately, but it is time to put them together. First, a fundamental axiom: *ideas will be effective only when the therapeutic alliance is solid.* My work with Patrick, an airline pilot, illustrates an error in timing: I attempted to force ideas in the absence of a solid therapeutic alliance.

Although his international travels made scheduling difficult, I had seen Patrick, a fifty-five-year-old airline pilot, for occasional consultations over a two-year period. When he was selected for a six-month special assignment to the flight office, we agreed to take advantage of his time on the ground to meet weekly.

Like most airline pilots, Patrick had been traumatized by recent chaos in the airline industry. The airline had slashed his salary in half, stripped away the pension he had been building for thirty years, and pushed him into flying so much that debilitating jet lag and circadian rhythm disruptions were causing him to suffer severe sleep disturbance, a condition exacerbated by incessant and incurable job-related tinnitus. His airline not only refused to assume responsibility for any of his problems but also, according to Patrick, was trying to force its pilots to fly even more.

His goals in therapy? Although Patrick still loved to fly, he knew that his health demanded a new career. What's more, he was unhappy about the lifeless live-in relationship in which he had languished for the past three years with his girlfriend, Marie. Patrick wanted either to improve the relationship or to end it and move out.

Therapy proceeded slowly. I struggled, unsuccessfully, to establish a strong therapeutic alliance, but Patrick was an airline captain accustomed to running his own show and, with his "top gun" military background, was cautious about revealing vulnerabilities. What's more, he had reason to be cautious, because almost any reported *DSM* diagnosis could ground him or possibly even cost him his Airline Transport Pilot certificate and therefore his job. With all these obstacles, Patrick remained distant in our sessions. I couldn't reach him. I knew he never looked forward to our hours, nor did he think about therapy between our meetings.

As for me, though I felt concern about Patrick, I couldn't bridge the distance between us. I rarely experienced pleasure seeing him and felt de-skilled and stymied in our work.

One day during our third month of therapy, Patrick developed sharp abdominal pain; he went to an emergency room, where a surgeon examined his abdomen, palpated an abdominal mass, and, with a look of great concern, immediately ordered a CT scan. In the four hours he waited for the scan, Patrick grew terrified of cancer, contemplated his death, and made several life-changing resolutions. Ultimately he learned that he had a benign cyst, which was corrected by surgery.

Still, those four hours contemplating death influenced Patrick in a remarkable way. In our next session, he was open to change as never before. He spoke, for example, of his shock at the thought of facing death with so very much unrealized potential for life. He knew now—really knew—that his work was physically harmful for him, and resolved to walk away from the job that had meant so much to him for so many years. He felt fortunate to have a fallback position—a standing invitation to work in his brother's retail business.

Patrick also resolved to repair a break with his father, which stemmed from a foolish argument many years ago and had continued to fester and contaminate his interactions with his entire family. Moreover, his long wait for the CT scan had increased Patrick's resolve to change his relationship with Maria. Either he would make a true effort to relate to her in a more affectionate and authentic manner, or he would leave her and seek a more compatible mate.

In the next weeks, therapy took on new vigor. Patrick was more open toward himself and even somewhat more open with me. He followed through on several of his resolutions: he reestablished connections with his father and entire family and attended a family Thanksgiving dinner, the first in a decade. He gave up flying and accepted, despite yet another cut in salary, a position as a manager of one of his brother's franchises. He procrastinated, however, about tackling his languishing relationship with Maria. After a few weeks, he began to regress, and his work in our sessions returned to its desultory nature.

With only three sessions remaining before he moved to another part of the country to begin his new job, I attempted to catalyze therapy and to move him back into the state of mind that had followed his confrontation with death. To that end, I sent him an e-mail, attaching my extensive notes of the post-emergency-room session in which he had become so open and resolved.

I have used the technique before with good results, helping patients reenter a previous state of mind. Moreover, for decades I have sent out written summaries of meetings to my group therapy patients. But, to my surprise, the approach entirely backfired. Patrick responded angrily to my e-mail: he interpreted my motives as punitive and saw only criticism in my act. He believed that I was haranguing him for having made no change in his relationship with Maria. Looking back, I realize now that I had never succeeded in establishing a sufficiently strong therapeutic alliance with Patrick. So, *nota bene,* in a distrustful or, especially, a competitive therapist-patient relationship, the best-intentioned and best-informed therapeutic efforts can fail because the patient may feel defeated by your observations and ultimately find a way to defeat you.

WORKING IN THE HERE-AND-NOW

I've often heard the question asked: does a person need a therapist if he or she has close friends? Intimate friends are essential to the good life. Furthermore, if one is surrounded by good friends or (more to the point) has the ability to form enduring intimate relationships, then one is far less likely to require therapy. What, then, is the difference between a good friend and a therapist? Good friends (or your hairdresser, masseuse, barber, or personal trainer) can be supportive and empathic. Good friends can be loving and caring confidants who can be counted on in time of need. But there remains one major difference: only therapists are likely to encounter you in the here-and-now.

Here-and-now interactions (that is, comments about the other's immediate behavior) seldom occur in social life. If they do, they are a sign of very great intimacy or of impending conflict (for example, "I don't like the way you're looking at me") or of a parent-child interaction ("Stop rolling your eyes when I'm talking to you").

In the therapy hour, the here-and-now is a focus on what is happening between the therapist and the patient in the immediate present. It is not a focus on the patient's historical past (the there-and-then) nor on the patient's current outside life (the there-and-now).

And why is the here-and-now important? A fundamental catechism of psychotherapy training is that the therapy situation is a social microcosm; that is, patients will sooner or later exhibit in the therapy situation the same behavior they exhibit in life outside. One who is self-effacing or arrogant or fearful or seductive or demanding will, sooner or later, show the same behavior toward the therapist during the therapy hour. At that point, a therapist can focus on the patient's role in the creation of the problematic issue occurring in the therapy relationship.

This is a first step in helping a patient assume responsibility for his or her life predicament. Ultimately, the patient is receptive to a fundamental corollary: if you are responsible for what has gone wrong in your life, then you, and only you, are able to change it.

What's more—and this is crucial—the information gleaned by the therapist in the here-and-now is exceedingly accurate. Although patients often talk a great deal about their interactions with others—lovers, friends, bosses, teachers, parents—you, the therapist, hear about those others (and their interactions with the patient) only through the eyes of your patient. Such accounts of outside events are indirect data, often skewed and highly unreliable.

How many times have I heard a patient describe another person—a spouse, for example—and then when I meet that spouse in a couples session, I shake my head in wonder. Is this lovely, vibrant person the same irritating or lifeless or uncaring individual I've been hearing about all these months? A therapist comes to know patients most fully through observing their behavior in the therapy sessions. This is by far your most trustworthy data: you have direct experience of the patient and how he or she interacts with you, and therefore how that patient is likely to interact with others.

Proper use of the here-and-now during therapy creates a safe laboratory, a comfortable arena in which patients can take risks, reveal their darkest and brightest selves, hear and accept feedback, and—most important of all—experiment with personal change. The more you focus on the here-and-now (and I make sure to do so in every single session), the tighter you and your patient are laced together in an intimate and trusting relationship.

Good therapy has a distinct cadence. Patients reveal feelings they have previously denied or suppressed. The therapist understands and accepts these dark or tender feelings. Bolstered by this acceptance, the patient feels safe and affirmed and takes even greater risks. The intimacy, the connectedness spawned by the here-and-now, keeps patients engaged in the therapy process; it provides an internal reference point to which a patient can look back and attempt to re-create in his or her social world.

Of course, a good relationship with one's therapist is not the ultimate goal of therapy. Patient and therapist almost never establish an enduring real-time friendship. But the patient's bond with the therapist serves as a dress rehearsal for the patient's outside social relationships.

I agree with Frieda Fromm-Reichman that therapists should strive to make every session memorable. The key to creating such a session is to harness the power of the here-and-now. I've discussed the technical approach to working in the here-and-now at great length elsewhere, so I'll turn here to only a few crucial steps in here-and-now work. Although some of these examples do not explicitly center on death anxiety, they will serve therapists in good stead by allowing them to increase connection with all patients they see, including those struggling with mortal fear.

Developing Sensitivity to the Here-and-Now

It was not difficult to focus on the here-and-now in my session with Mark. First, I simply inquired into his comment that he habitually thought of Ruth on the way to see me and, later, I reflected on his change of behavior in the session (that is, his posing several personal questions to me). But often a therapist will need to search for more subtle transitions.

After years of practice, I've developed norms for various behaviors in my therapy setting and am alert to departures from the norm. Consider something as seemingly trivial and irrelevant as parking. For the last fifteen years, my office has been a cottage two hundred feet in front of my home, which has a long, narrow driveway to the street. Although there is ample room for parking in a lot between home and office, I occasionally notice that a patient habitually parks far away on the street.

I find it useful, at some point, to inquire about that choice. One patient answered that he did not want his car seen parked near my home because he feared that someone, perhaps a visitor to my home, would recognize his car and realize he was seeing a shrink. Another stated she did not want to intrude on my privacy. Still another was embarrassed by my seeing his expensive Masserati. Each of these reasons was clearly relevant to the therapeutic relationship.

Moving from Outside to Inside Material

Experienced therapists are on the alert for the here-and-now equivalent of any issue raised in the session. Navigating from the patient's outside life or distant past to the here-and-now increases the level of engagement and effectiveness of the work. A session with Ellen, a forty-year-old woman whom I had started seeing a year earlier for death panics, illustrates a navigational strategy.

THE WOMAN WHO WOULDN'T COMPLAIN: ELLEN Ellen began a session by saying she had almost called to cancel because she felt ill.

"How bad are you feeling now?" I asked.

She shrugged it off, "I'm better."

"Tell me what happens at home when you're ill," I asked.

"My husband doesn't do much caretaking. He usually doesn't even notice."

"What do you do? How do you let him know?"

"I've never been a complainer. But I wouldn't mind his doing something for me when I'm sick."

"So you want some caretaking, but you want it to happen without asking for it or signaling you need it?"

She nodded.

I had many options at this point. I could, for example, have explored her husband's lack of caretaking or looked into her past history of illness. I chose instead to shift into the here-and-now.

"So, tell me, Ellen, how does that work here with me? You don't do much complaining in this office even though I'm officially your caretaker."

"I told you I almost canceled today because of illness."

"But when I asked how you felt, you shrugged it off without further comment. I wonder what it would be like if you really complained and really told me what you wanted from me."

"That would be like begging," she responded instantly.

"Begging? And yet you pay me to take care of you? Tell me more about begging. What does 'begging' evoke?"

"I had four siblings, and home lesson 101 was not to complain. I can still hear my stepfather's voice: 'Grow up—you can't keep on whining all your life.' I can't even begin to tell you how often I heard that from him. My mother reinforced this; she felt lucky to have remarried and did not want us upsetting him. We were unwanted baggage, and he was so mean and so harsh. The last thing I wanted to do was to draw his attention."

"So, then, in this office you come for help, and yet you mute your complaints. This conversation is bringing to mind the time a few months ago when you had that neck problem and wore a cervical collar but never discussed it. I recall being confused about whether or not you were in pain. You never complain. But, tell me, if you *were* to complain to me, what do you think I would feel or say?"

Ellen smoothed her flower patterned skirt—she was always immaculately dressed, well groomed, scrubbed clean—and, closing her eyes, drew a deep breath and said, "I had a dream two or three weeks ago that I never told you. I was in your bathroom, and menstrual blood was flowing. I couldn't stop it. I couldn't clean myself. It was on my socks and seeped through to my sneakers. You were in the office next door but didn't ask what was happening. Then I heard some voices in there. Maybe it was your next client or some friends or your wife."

The dream portrayed her concerns about shameful, dirty, concealed parts that would ultimately leak out in therapy. But she viewed me as indifferent: I didn't ask what was wrong, was too busy with another client or with friends, and was neither willing nor able to help.

After Ellen was able to tell me about this dream, we entered a new, constructive phase of therapy in which she explored her feelings of distrust and fear of men and her fear of closeness with me.

This vignette illustrates an important principle of here-and-now navigation: when a patient brings up a life issue, search for the here-and-now equivalent, some way the issue can be brought into the therapy relationship. When Ellen brought up the issue of her illness and her husband's lack of caretaking, I immediately zeroed in on caretaking in our therapy.

Checking Frequently on the Here-and-Now

I make a point of checking on the here-and-now at least once a session. Sometimes I simply say, "We're close to the end of the hour, and I'd like to focus a bit on how the two of us are doing today. How do you feel about the space between us today?" Or "How much distance is there between us today?" Sometimes nothing comes of this. But even so, the invitation is made and the norm established that we examine everything transpiring between us.

But often something will come of this query, especially if I add some observations—for example, "I notice that we're circling the same things we talked about last week. Do you feel that way too?" Or "I've noticed you haven't mentioned your death anxiety for the past couple of weeks. Why do you think that is so? Is it possible that you think it's too much for me?" Or "I had a feeling we were very close at the beginning of the session, but we've backed away the last twenty minutes. Do you agree? Is that your observation too?"

Psychotherapy training today is so often directed toward brief and structured therapy that many young therapists may consider my focus on the here-and-now relationship as irrelevant or too precious, or even bizarre. "Why so self-referential?" they often ask. "Why refer everything back to the unreal relationship with the therapist? After all, we're not in the business of preparing the patient for a life in therapy. There's a tough world out there in which patients face competition, strife, harshness." And the answer is, of course, as the case of Patrick suggests, that the positive therapeutic alliance is a prerequisite for the effectiveness of any therapy. It is not the end, but a means to the end. A major internal shift can occur when patients form a genuine, trusting relationship with the therapist, disclose everything and still be accepted and supported. Such patients experience new parts of themselves, parts previously denied or distorted. They begin to value themselves and their own perceptions rather than overvaluing the perceptions of others. Patients transform the therapist's positive regard into personal self-regard. Moreover, they develop a new internal standard for the quality of a genuine relationship. The intimacy with the therapist serves as an internal reference point. Knowing they have the ability to form relationships, they develop the confidence and willingness to form similarly good relationships in the future.

Learning to Use Your Own Here-and-Now Feelings

Your most valuable tool as a therapist is your own reaction to your patient. If you feel intimidated, angry, seduced, bewildered, bewitched, or any of myriad other feelings, you should take these reactions very seriously. They are important data, and you must search for a way to turn them to good use in therapy.

But first, as I suggest to student therapists, you have to determine the source of those feelings. To what extent are your own idiosyncratic or neurotic issues shaping your feelings? In other words, are you an accurate observer? Do your feelings provide information about the patient or about yourself? Here, of course, we are entering the domain of transference and counter-transference.

When a patient responds in some inappropriate irrational manner to the therapist, we term that transference. A clear example of the distortion involved in transference is the patient who—on apparently no basis—strongly distrusts a therapist who is characteristically trusted by other patients; furthermore, the patient has a pattern of distrusting most males in a position of some expertise or authority. (The term *transference,* of course, refers to Freud's view that important feelings about adults in early childhood are "transferred," or cast, onto someone else.)

Conversely, the opposite can happen: therapists can have distorted views of their clients—that is, the therapist sees a client in a distorted fashion, far different from the way others (including other therapists) see that same person. This phenomenon is referred to as countertransference.

You need to distinguish between the two. Does the patient have a tendency for great interpersonal distortion? Or is the therapist an angry, confused, defensive person (or perhaps one who is having a very bad day) who views patients through distorted lenses? Of course it is not an all or none phenomenon—elements of transference and countertransference may coexist.

I never tire of telling student therapists that their most vital instrument is their own self, and that, consequently, the instrument must be finely honed. Therapists must have a great deal of self-knowledge, must trust their observations, and must relate to their clients in a caring and professional manner. It is precisely for this reason that personal therapy is (or should be) at the core of every therapy training program. I believe not only that therapists should have years of personal therapy (including group therapy) during their training but also that they should return to therapy as they progress through life. Once you feel confident about yourself as a therapist, about your observations and objectivity, you become more free to use, with confidence, your feelings about your patients.

"I'm Very Disappointed In You": Naomi A session with Naomi, a sixty-eight-year-old retired English teacher with high death anxiety, severe hypertension, and many somatic complaints, illustrates many of the issues involved in disclosing your here-and-now feelings. One day she entered my office with her usual warm smile, sat down, and, with her head held high, looked straight at me and, without a waver in her voice, launched into a surprising diatribe:

"I am disappointed in the way you reacted to me last session. Extremely disappointed. You weren't present with me, you did not give me what I needed, you had no appreciation how awful it might feel to a woman my age to have such debilitating GI problems or how it might feel for me to discuss it. I left the session thinking of an incident a few years ago. I saw my dermatologist for a nasty lesion on my vagina, and he invited all his medical students to come see the sight. It was a horror. Well, that's just how I felt last session. You failed to meet my standards."

I was stunned. Pondering how best to respond, I quickly went over the last session in my mind. (I had, of course, read my notes before she entered.) My take on the previous hour was so very different: I had thought it an excellent session and that I had done good work. Naomi had done heavy-duty revealing of her discouragement about her aging body and such GI problems as gas, constipation, and hemorrhoids, and of the difficulty of giving herself an enema and her recall of enemas as a child. These were not easy things to talk about, and I told her I admired her willingness to bring them up. Because she had thought that some new medications for her cardiac arrhythmia had caused her symptoms, I had taken out my *Physicians' Desk Reference* during the session and reviewed the side effects of the drugs with her. I recalled feeling empathy for her having yet a new ordeal in addition to a long list of other medical problems.

So what to do? Engage her in an analysis of the previous session? Look at her idealized expectations of me? Look at our very different perceptions of the previous hour? But there was something more pressing—my own feelings. I had a surge of great irritation toward

Naomi: there she was, I thought, sitting up on her throne and passing out judgment of me with zero regard for how I might feel.

Moreover, this was not the first time. In our three years of therapy, she had begun sessions like this several times, but never before had it irritated me quite so much. Perhaps it was because during the last week I had taken time between sessions to investigate her problems and had spoken to a friend, a gastroenterologist, about her symptoms—but had not yet had time to mention this to her.

I decided it was important to let Naomi know how I felt. For one thing, I knew she'd pick up on my feelings: she was exceptionally perceptive. But also I had no doubt that if I were irritated with her, others in her life surely were as well. Because it may be devastating for a patient to hear of a therapist's irritation, I tried to proceed gently.

"Naomi, I feel surprised and unsettled at your comments. You say these things so . . . so . . . uh . . . imperiously. I thought I worked hard last week to give you all I could. Moreover, it's not the first time you've begun the session in this highly critical manner. And another thing to throw into this mix is that you've opened many other sessions in the exact opposite manner. I mean that you've expressed gratitude for an amazing session that sometimes puzzled me, since I hadn't remembered that session as so extraordinary."

Naomi looked alarmed. Her pupils were huge. "Are you saying I'm not supposed to tell you my feelings?"

"No, by no means. Neither of us should censor ourselves. We should both share feelings and then analyze them. I'm particularly struck, though, by your manner. There are different ways you might have spoken. You might, for example, have said that we weren't working together well last week, or that you felt distant or—"

"Look," her voice was strident, "I felt pissed at my body falling apart bit by bit, I have two stents in my coronary arteries, I have a pacemaker ticking away, an artificial hip, and my other hip is killing me, the meds are bloating me up like a pig, and my gas makes it humiliating to go out in public. Do I have to tiptoe around here?"

"I'm aware of your feelings about what's happening to your body. I do feel your pain and said as much last week."

"And what do you mean by 'imperiously'?"

"The way you looked right at me and spoke as though you were passing a sentence. It seemed to me you had not the slightest concern about how your words would make me feel."

Her face darkened. "As for my language and carriage and the way I spoke to you"—and here she practically hissed—"well, you had it coming. You had it coming."

"A lot of feeling there, Naomi," I said.

"Well, I'm very upset by your criticisms. I've always felt so free here—this is the one place I was able to speak freely. Now you're telling me that if I get angry, I should muzzle myself. That upsets me. That's not the way our therapy has worked. Not the way it should work."

"I never said I want you to muzzle yourself. But surely you want to know the impact of your words on me. You don't, I think, want me to muzzle myself. After all, your words have consequences."

"What do you mean?"

"Well, your words at the beginning of the session make me feel more distant from you. Is that what you want?"

"Explain more. You're speaking in sound bites."

"Here's the dilemma: I know you want me to be close and intimate with you—you've said that many times. Yet your words make me wary, make me feel I need to be careful about getting too close to you lest I get bitten."

"Now everything will be different here," Naomi said, her head slumping. "It will never be the same."

"You mean that the feelings I have at this moment are irrevocable? Locked in cement? Remember last year when your friend Marjorie was angry with you for insisting on going to a certain movie, and how panicked you were at the thought she would never, never speak to you again? Well, as you've seen, feelings can change.

You and she talked it out and resumed your friendship. In fact, I believe the two of you became even closer. Remember, too, that the situation in this room is even more conducive to working through things because, unlike elsewhere, we have a special set of rules—that is, to keep on communicating no matter what.

"But Naomi," I continued, "I'm getting away from your anger. When you said 'you had it coming,' that was pretty intense. That came from deep down."

"I'm amazed myself," she replied, "how strong that came over me. The anger, no . . . more than anger—fury—just burst out of me."

"Just here with me? Or elsewhere, too?"

"No, no, it's *not* just here with you. It's leaking out all over the place. Yesterday my niece was driving me to the doctor, and there was a stalled gardener's truck blocking the way. I got so angry at the driver I felt like pounding him. I went looking for him but couldn't find him. And then I got angry at my niece for not driving around the truck and passing it—even if it meant jumping the curb. She said there wasn't enough room. I insisted, and we got into such an argument that we got out of the car, and she measured the distance with her footsteps and showed me there was not enough room because of the parked cars on the road. Moreover, the curbs were too high to jump. She kept saying, 'Calm down, Aunt Naomi, it's the gardener trying to do his job. He's not happy about this, and he's trying to do something about it.' And I couldn't help myself. I was enraged at the driver and kept saying to myself, 'How could he do this to me? He's not up to standard.'

"And, of course, my niece was right. The driver rushed back with two helpers, and they pushed the truck out of way so we could pass, and I felt humiliated—a sputtering old lady. Anger everywhere—to waiters for not bringing my iced tea fast enough, to the parking attendant for being so slow, to the movie cashier for fumbling so long making change and giving me my ticket; hell, I could've sold a car in that period of time."

The hour was up. "I'm sorry to end now, Naomi. Such strong feelings today. I know it's not been comfortable for you, but it's important work. Let's continue this next week. We've got to put our heads together to figure out why so much anger is emerging."

Naomi agreed, but phoned the next day to say that she felt too wobbly to wait another week, so we scheduled a session for the following day.

She started out in an unusual way: "Perhaps you know the Dylan Thomas poem, 'Do Not Go Gentle.'"

Before I could answer, she recited the first lines:

Do not go gentle into that good night,
Old age should burn and rave at close of day;
Rage, rage against the dying of the light.
Though wise men at their end know dark is right,
Because their words had forked no lightning they
Do not go gentle into that good night.

"I could go on," Naomi said. "I know it by heart, but . . ." She paused.

Oh, please, please go on, I thought to myself. She had recited the lines beautifully, and there are few things I love more than listening to poetry read aloud. How odd to be paid for this treat.

"These lines contain the answer to your—or our—question about my anger," Naomi continued. "Last night, as I was thinking about our session, this poem just popped into my mind. Funny, I taught this poem to my eleventh-grade English students for years, but never really thought about the meaning of the words—or, at least, I never applied them to me."

"I think I see where you're heading," I said, "but I'd rather hear it from you."

"I think . . . no, I mean I'm absolutely certain that my rage is really about my situation in life: my diminishment and my death not far ahead. Everything is being taken away from me—my hip, my bowel function, my libido, my power, my hearing and eyesight. I'm weak, I'm defenseless, and I'm waiting for death. So I'm following Dylan Thomas's instruction: I'm not going gentle, I'm raving and raging at the close of my day. And my pathetic, impotent words are sure forking no lightning. I don't want to die. And I guess I must think raging will help. But maybe the only real function of raging is to inspire great poetry."

In subsequent sessions we focused more heavily and effectively on the terror behind the anger. Naomi's (and Dylan Thomas's) strategy for quelling death anxiety helped counter her sense of diminishment and powerlessness, yet it soon backfired as it disrupted her sense of connectedness with her vital inner circle of support. Truly effective therapy has to attend not only to the visible symptom (anger, in this instance) but to the underlying terror of death from which such symptoms erupt.

I took a chance when I described Naomi's manner as imperious and reminded her of the consequences of her words. But I had a large margin of safety: we had established a close, trusting connection over a long time. Because no one likes to hear negative comments, perhaps especially from a therapist, I took several steps to ensure acceptance. I used language that would not offend her: to say, for example, that I felt "distanced" implied my underlying wish to be closer and intimate, and who can take offense at that?

Furthermore (and this is important), I was not globally critical of her: I made a point of commenting only on pieces of behavior. I stated, in effect, that when she behaved in such and such a manner, I ended up feeling such and such. And then I quickly added that this was counter to her interests, as she clearly did not want me to feel distanced and unsettled or fearful of her.

Note my emphasis on empathy in Naomi's treatment. It is vital for the effective, connected therapy relationship. In my earlier discussion of Carl Rogers's ideas about effective therapist behavior, I emphasized the role of the therapist's accurate empathy (along with unconditional positive regard and genuineness). But work on empathy is *bidirectional:* not only must you experience the patient's world, but you *must also help patients develop their own empathy for others.*

One effective approach is to ask, "How do you think your comment makes me feel?" Thus I was careful to let Naomi know about the consequences of her comments. Her first response, emerging out of her anger, was "you had it coming"; but later, when she looked back on her words, she was disturbed by her own vitriolic tone and comments. Uncomfortable that she had evoked negative feelings in me, she feared that she had jeopardized the safe supportive space of our therapy.

THERAPIST SELF-DISCLOSURE

Therapists should reveal themselves—as I tried to do with Naomi. Therapist self-disclosure is a complex and contested area. Few suggestions I make to therapists are as unsettling as my urging them to reveal more of themselves. It sets their teeth on edge. It evokes the specter of a patient invading their personal life. I'll address all these objections in detail, but let me begin by stating that I do not mean that therapists should reveal themselves indiscriminately: to begin with they should reveal only when the revelation will be of value to the patient.

Bear in mind that therapist self-disclosure is not one-dimensional. The discussion of Naomi centers on therapist disclosure in the here-and-now. But, in addition, there are two other categories of therapist self-disclosure: disclosure about the mechanism of therapy and disclosure about a therapist's personal life, past or present.

Disclosure About the Mechanism of Therapy

Should we be open and transparent about the way therapy helps? Dostoevsky's Grand Inquisitor believes that what mankind really wants is "magic, mystery and authority." Indeed, early healers and religious figures supplied those ineffable commodities in great abundance. Shamans were masters of magic and mystery. Former generations of physicians bedecked themselves in long white coats, adopted an all-knowing manner and bedazzled patients with impressive prescriptions written in Latin. More recently, therapists have continued—with their reticence, their deep-sounding interpretations, their diplomas and pictures of various teachers and gurus lining their office walls—to stay apart from and above their clients.

Even today some therapists provide patients only a sketchy description of how therapy works because they accept Freud's belief that ambiguity and the therapist's opacity encourages the formation of transference. Freud considered transference important because an investigation of the transference provides valuable information about the patient's inner world and early life experience.

I believe, however, that a therapist has everything to gain and nothing to lose by being entirely transparent about the process of therapy. Considerable persuasive research in both individual and group therapy has documented that therapists who systematically and thoroughly prepare patients for therapy have better outcomes. As for transference, I believe it is a hardy organism and will grow robustly even in broad daylight.

So I am personally transparent about the mechanism of therapy. I tell patients about how therapy works, about my role in the process, and, most important of all, what they can do to facilitate their own therapy. If it seems indicated, I have no hesitation about suggesting selected publications about therapy.

I make a point of clarifying the here-and-now focus and, even in the first session, ask about how the patient and I are doing in it. I ask such questions as "What expectations you have of me? How do I fit or not fit those expectations?" "Do we seem on track?" "Do you have feelings about me that we should explore?"

I follow such questions by saying something like this: "You'll find that I do this often. I ask such here-and-now questions because I believe that the exploration of our relationship will provide us valuable and accurate information. You can tell me about issues arising with friends or your boss or your spouse, but always there is a limitation: I don't know them, and you can't help but give me information that reflects your own bias. We all do that; we can't help it. But what goes on here in this office is reliable because we both experience and can work on that information immediately." All my patients have understood this explanation and accepted it.

Disclosure About the Therapist's Personal Life

Open the door a crack on their personal life, some therapists fear, and patients will relentlessly ask for more. "How happy are you?" "How is your marriage going? Your social life? Your sexual life?"

This is, in my experience, a bogus fear. Although I encourage patients to ask questions, no patient has ever insisted on knowing uncomfortably intimate details of my life. If that were to happen, I would respond by focusing on the process; that is, I would inquire about the patient's motivation in pressing or embarrassing me. Again, I emphasize to therapists, reveal yourself when it enhances therapy, not because of pressure from the patient or because of your own needs or rules.

However richly such disclosure may contribute to therapy's effectiveness, it is a complex act, as we see in this narrative of a session with James, the forty-six-year-old man described in Chapter Three, who was sixteen when his brother was killed in an automobile accident.

JAMES ASKS A DIFFICULT QUESTION Although two of my most fundamental values as a therapist are tolerance and unconditional acceptance, I still have my prejudices. My bête noir is bizarre belief: aura therapy; semi-deified gurus; hands-on healers; prophets; untested healing claims of various nutritionists; aroma therapy, homeopathy, and zany ideas about such things as astral traveling, healing power of crystals, religious miracles, angels, feng shui, channeling, remote viewing, meditational levitation, psychokinesis, poltergeists, past lives therapy, and UFOs and extraterrestrials who inspired early civilizations, designed patterns in wheat fields, and built the Egyptian pyramids.

Still, I've always believed that I could put all prejudices aside and work with anyone regardless of his or her belief systems. But the day that James, with his fervid passion for the paranormal, entered my office, I knew that my therapeutic neutrality was to be severely tested.

Although James did not seek therapy because of his paranormal beliefs, some issues surrounding them surfaced in almost every session. Consider our work on this dream:

I am soaring through the air. I visit my father in Mexico City, glide over the city and look in through the window of his bedroom. I see him weeping, and I know without asking that he is weeping about me, about having abandoned me

when I was a child. Next I find myself in the Guadalajara
cemetery where my brother is buried. For some reason, I
call my own cell phone number and hear my message, "I'm
James G . . . I'm in pain. Please send help."

In discussing this dream, James spoke bitterly of
his father who had abandoned the family when James
was a child. He wasn't sure if his father was alive; the
last James had heard, he was living somewhere in Mexico City. Not once could James remember having received a tender fatherly word or gift from him.

"So," I said, after we had discussed the dream for a
few minutes, "the dream seems to be expressing your
hope for something from your father, some sign that he
thinks about you, that he has remorse for not having
been a better father.

"And that cell phone message asking for help!" I
continued. "What strikes me is that you've often described your difficulty asking for help. In fact, you said
the other week that I am the only person that you have
ever explicitly asked for help. But in the dream you're
more open about needing help. So is the dream portraying a change? Is it saying something about you and
me? Perhaps some parallel between what you get or
want from me and what you yearned for from your
father?

"And then in the dream you visit your brother's
grave. Your thoughts about that? Are you now asking
for help in dealing with your brother's death?"

James agreed that my caring for him had ignited his awareness and yearning for what he had never gotten from his father. And he agreed also that he had changed since starting therapy: he was more readily sharing his problems with his wife and his mother.

But then he added, "You're suggesting one way to look at the dream. I'm not saying it's unsound; I'm not saying it's not a useful way. But I have an alternate explanation that's far more real to me. I believe what you call a dream is not really a dream. It's a memory, a record of my astral traveling last night to my father's home and to my brother's grave."

I took care not to roll my eyes or cup my head in my hands. I wondered whether he'd say that calling his own cell phone was a memory also, but I felt sure that entrapping him cleverly or airing our difference in beliefs would be counterproductive. Instead, having disciplined myself over our months of therapy to suppress my skepticism, I tried to enter his world and imagine what it would be like to live in a world with hovering spirits and astral traveling, and I also attempted a gentle exploration of the psychological origins and history of his beliefs.

Later in the session, he discussed his shame about his drinking and his sloth and said that he will feel mortified when he meets his grandparents and his brother in a reunion in heaven.

A couple of minutes later, he noted, "I saw you squinting when I spoke about my reunion with my grandparents."

"I wasn't aware of squinting, James."

"I saw it! And I think you squinted earlier when I spoke of my astral traveling. Tell me the truth, Irv: What was your reaction to what I said just now about heaven?"

I could have evaded the question, as we therapists often do, by reflecting on the process of his asking it, but I decided that my best route was to be entirely honest. He had, without doubt, picked up many cues about my skepticism; to deny them would be anti-therapy by undermining his (accurate) view of reality.

"James, I'll tell you what I can about what was going on in me. When you spoke about how your grandfather and brother knew everything about your life now, I was startled. These aren't my beliefs. But what I tried to do as you spoke was to try hard to plunge into your experience, to imagine what it might be like to live in a world of spirits, a world in which your dead relatives know all about your life and your thoughts."

"Don't you believe in an afterlife?"

"I don't. But I also feel we can never be certain of such things. I imagine it offers great comfort to you, and I'm all for anything that offers you peace of mind, life satisfaction, and encourages a virtuous life. But, personally, I don't find the idea of a reunion in heaven credible. I consider it as stemming from a wish."

"Then what religion do you believe in?"

"I don't believe in any religion or any god. I have an entirely secular view of life."

"But how is it possible to live like that? Without a set of ordained morals. How can life be tolerable or have any meaning without the idea of improving your position in the next life?"

I began to grow uneasy about where this discussion would lead and whether I was serving James's best interests. All in all, however, I decided it was best to continue being forthright.

"My real interest is in *this* life and in improving it for myself and others. Let me speak to your puzzlement about how I can find meaning without religion. I disagree about religion being the source of meaning and morality. I don't think there is an essential connection—or let me at least say an *exclusive* connection—between religion, meaning, and morality. I think I live a fulfilling and virtuous life. I am fully dedicated to helping others, like you for example, to live a more satisfying life. I would say I get my meaning in life from this human world right here, right now. I think my meaning comes from helping others find their meaning. I believe that preoccupation with a next life may undermine full participation in this life."

James looked so interested that I continued on for a few minutes to describe some of my recent readings in Epicurus and Nietzsche that emphasized this very point. I mentioned how Nietzsche much admired Christ but felt that Paul and later Christian leaders diluted Christ's real message and drained this current life of meaning. In fact, I pointed out, Nietzsche had much hostility toward Socrates and Plato because of their disdain of the body, their emphasis on the soul's immortality, and their concentration on preparing for the next life. These very beliefs were cherished by the Neo-Platonists and eventually permeated early Christian eschatology.

I stopped and looked at James, expecting some challenging response. Suddenly, to my great astonishment, he began to weep. I handed him Kleenex after Kleenex and waited until his sobs stopped.

"Try to keep talking to me, James. What do the tears say?"

"They say, 'I've been waiting so long for this conversation . . . have waited so long to have a serious intellectual conversation about things that have depth.' Everything around me, our whole culture—TV, video games, porno—is so dumbed down. Everything I do at work, all the minutia of contracts and lawsuits and divorce mediation—it's all money, it's all shit, it's all about nothing, all so meaningless."

James thus was influenced not by our content but by our process—that is, by my taking him seriously. He considered my expression of my own ideas and beliefs as a gift, and our vast ideological differences proved entirely inconsequential. We agreed to disagree; he brought me a book about UFOs, and I, in turn, offered him a book by the contemporary skeptic Richard Dawkins. Our relationship, my caring, and my giving him what he failed to get from his father proved to be the crucial factor in our therapy. As I pointed out in Chapter Three, he improved greatly in many ways, but finished therapy with his paranormal beliefs unchallenged and intact.

Pushed to the Limits of Self-Disclosure

Amelia is a fifty-one-year-old black, heavy-set, highly intelligent yet shy public health nurse. Thirty-five years before I saw her, she had been, for two long years, a homeless heroin addict and (to support her habit) a prostitute. I believe anyone spotting her then on the streets of Harlem—a ragged, emaciated, demoralized soldier in the vast army of homeless heroin-addicted prostitutes—would have laid good odds that she was doomed. Yet, with the help of a forced detoxification during six months in prison—along with Narcotics Anonymous, extraordinary courage, and a ferocious will to live—Amelia changed her life and her identity, moved to the West Coast and began a career as a club singer. She had enough talent for regular paying gigs to put herself through high school and, later, nursing school. For the last twenty-five years, she had devoted herself entirely to work in hospices and shelters for the poor and homeless.

In our first session, I learned that she suffered from severe insomnia. Typically she would be awakened by a nightmare, very few of which she remembered, except for scraps involving being chased and running for her life. She then was so anxious about death that she rarely fell back asleep. When it got so bad that she dreaded going to bed, she decided to get help. Having recently read a story I had written, "In Search of the Dreamer," she thought I could help her.

The first time she entered my office she plopped herself in my chair, saying she hoped she wouldn't fall asleep on me because she was exhausted, having been up much of the night recovering from a nightmare. Usually, she said, she could not remember dreams, but this one had stayed with her.

I am lying down looking at my curtains. They are made of rosy-red pleats with yellowish light coming through between the pleats. The reddish stripes are wider than the stripes of light. But what is strange is this curtain is linked to music. I mean, instead of light coming through, I hear the strains of an old Roberta Flack song, "Killing Me Softly," pouring through the light stripes. I used to sing this song a lot around Oakland clubs when I was in college. In the dream I became frightened by the way the light was being replaced by music. Then suddenly the music stops and I know the music-maker is coming for me. I woke up really scared around four A.M. That was the end of sleep for that night.

It was not only her nightmares and insomnia that drove her to therapy. She had a second significant problem: she wanted a relationship with a man and had started several relationships, but none, she said, had ever really gotten off the ground.

For the first few sessions I explored her history, her fears of death, and her memories of close escapes from death during her years as a prostitute, but I sensed enormous resistance. Her affect was always muted. She seemed to have no conscious anxiety about death; on the contrary, she had chosen to do a great deal of hospice work.

During the first three months of therapy, the mere process of speaking to me and sharing for the first time details of her life on the streets seemed comforting, and her sleep improved. She knew she continued to dream, but was never able to recall more than small snippets.

Her fear of intimacy was immediately evident in our therapy relationship. She rarely looked at me, and I experienced a wide gulf between us. Earlier in this chapter, I discussed the significance of my patients' parking patterns. Of all my patients, Amelia parked farthest away.

Keeping in mind the lesson I learned from Patrick (discussed earlier in this chapter), that ideas lose their effectiveness in the absence of an intimate trusting connection, I resolved over the next few months to work on her problems of intimacy, and particularly focused on her relationship with me. Movement, however, occurred at a glacial pace until the following memorable session.

As she walked into my office, she received a cell phone call and asked if it was okay to take it. She then had a brief phone conversation about a meeting later that day, using language that was so formal and perfunctory that I thought she was speaking to her boss. As soon as she hung up, I asked and learned that no, it was not her boss but her most recent boyfriend, with whom she was making dinner arrangements.

"There's got to be a difference between talking to him and to your boss," I said. "How about some term of endearment. Honey? Sweetheart? Sugar?"

She looked at me as if I were a drop-in from a parallel universe and changed the subject to tell me about attending a recent Narcotics Anonymous group meeting the day before. (Though she had been abstinent for over thirty years, she still attended periodic NA or AA meetings.) The meeting was held in a section of town highly reminiscent of the Harlem neighborhood she had frequented during her life as an addict and prostitute. On the walk to the meeting though a drug-infested neighborhood, she, as always, experienced an odd nostalgia and found herself searching for doorways and alleys that might offer a place to spend the night.

"It's not that I want to be back there, Doctor Yalom."

"You still call me Doctor Yalom, and I call you Amelia," I interrupted. "That doesn't seem balanced."

"Like I said, give me time. Got to know you better. But, as I was saying, whenever I go to these . . . uh . . .

seedy sections of town, I keep having waves of feelings that are not entirely negative. Hard to describe them but . . . I don't know . . . it's like . . . homesickness."

"Homesickness? What do you make of that, Amelia?"

"Not sure myself. Tell you what I always hear: a voice saying in my head saying, 'I did it.' I always hear that. 'I did it.'"

"Sounds like you're saying to yourself, 'I went through hell and back and I survived'"

"Yeah, something like that. There's something else too. You may find this hard to believe, but life was so much simpler and easier back then on the street. No worrying about budgets and meetings, or training new nurses who get freaked out in a week. No hassle with cars, furniture, tax deductions. No worrying what I can legally do for folks and what I can't. No kissing doctors' asses. When I was on the Harlem streets, all I had to think about was one thing. One thing only—the next sack of dope. And, of course, where the next john was coming from to pay for it. Life was simple, day-to-day, minute-to-minute survival."

"A little selective memory going on here, Amelia. How about the filth, the freezing nights on the streets, the broken bottles, the men who stiffed you, the brutal men who raped you, the odors of urine and spilled beer? And death lurking everywhere—the dead bodies you saw, and you almost getting murdered? You don't hold those things in mind."

"Yeah, yeah, I know. You're right, I forget about those. And I forgot about them then when they happened. Almost killed by some freak and then next minute I was back on the street."

"As I recall, you saw a friend thrown off the roof of a building and came close to being murdered yourself three times—I remember that harrowing story you told me about being chased through the park by this maniac with a knife and kicking off your shoes and running barefooted for a half hour. Yet each time you went right back to work. It's as though heroin put all other thoughts out of mind. Even the fear of death."

"Right. Like I said I was only thinking one thought—the next sack of heroin. I didn't think about death. Had no fears of death."

"Yet now death comes back to haunt you in your dreams."

"Yeah, it is strange. And so is this . . . this . . . homesickness."

"Does pride enter into this?" I asked. "You've got to feel proud about climbing out of there."

"Some of that. But, not enough, you'd say. I don't have free thinking time. My mind is loaded to the hilt with numbers and work and sometimes Hal [the boyfriend]. And staying alive, I guess. Staying out of drugs."

"Does coming here and seeing me help you stay alive? Keep you away from drugs?"

"My whole life, my work in groups, my therapy also, helps."

"That wasn't my question, Amelia. Do *I* help you stay off drugs?"

"I said it. I said you help. Everything helps."

"That throw-in phrase 'everything helps'—can you see how that dilutes things? Takes something away from us? Keeps us distant? You avoid me. Can you try to talk more about feelings you have about me—in this session so far or in last week's session or perhaps thoughts about me during the week?"

"Oh no. Man, you off on that again?"

"Trust me—it's important, Amelia."

"You telling me all patients think about their therapist?"

"Yes, exactly. That's my experience. I know I sure had a lot of thoughts about my therapist."

Amelia had been slumping in her chair, making herself smaller as she always did when I turned the discussion to us, but now she straightened up. I had gotten her full attention.

"Your therapy? When? What thoughts did you have?"

"I saw a good guy, psychologist about fifteen years ago. Rollo May. I looked forward to our sessions. I liked his gentleness, his attentiveness to everything. I liked the way he dressed with turtlenecks and a necklace of turquoise Indian jewelry. I liked his saying

to me that we had a special relationship because we had
the same professional interests. I loved his reading the
draft of one of my books and complimenting me on it."

Silence. Amelia remained motionless, staring out
the window.

"And you?" I asked. "Your turn."

"Well, I guess I like your gentleness too." She
squirmed and looked away while saying this.

"Keep going. Say more."

"It's embarrassing."

"I know. But embarrassment means we're saying
something important to each other. I think embarrassment is our target, our quarry—we've got to work
right through it. So let's plunge right into the middle of
your embarrassment. Try to keep going."

"Well, I liked the time you helped me on with my
coat. I also liked your chuckling those times when I
fixed the turned-up corner of the rug. Man, I don't
know why that don't bother you too. You could do some
fixing up of your office. That desk of yours is a mess . . .
okay, okay, I'll stay on track. I remember the time that
dentist gave me a bottle of fifty Vicodin and how hard
you tried to get me to give it to you. I mean the dentist
drops it in my lap—you think I'm gonna give it away? I
remember at the end of that session when you wouldn't
let go of my hand when I tried to bolt out of the
office. I tell you one thing, I'm grateful that you
didn't put therapy on the line—give me an ultimatum
that it was that bottle of Vicodin or you'd stop therapy.

Other therapists would have done that. And I tell you what—I would have left them. Left you, too."

"I like your saying these things, Amelia. I'm moved, I'm touched by it. What's the last few minutes like for you?"

"Embarrassing, that's all."

"Why?"

"Because now I am open to be mocked."

"Did that ever happen?"

Amelia then discussed some incidents from her early childhood and adolescence in which she was mocked. They did not seem too striking to me, and I wondered aloud whether her embarrassment was rooted instead in her dark heroin days. She disagreed, as she had on other occasions, and stated that embarrassment problems long preceded her drug use. Then, becoming pensive, she turned and looked directly at me and said, "I have a question for you."

That caught my attention. She had never said that before. I had no idea what to expect and waited eagerly. I love such moments.

"Not sure you'll be willing to handle this, but here it is. You ready?"

I nodded.

"Would you welcome me as a member of your family? I mean, you know what I mean. Theoretically."

I took some time on this one. I wanted to be honest and genuine. I looked at her: her head held high, her large eyes fixed on me, not avoiding me as they usually did. Her glistening brown skin on her forehead and cheeks looked so freshly scrubbed. I examined my feelings carefully and said: "The answer is yes, Amelia. I consider you a courageous person. And a lovely person. I'm full of admiration for what you've overcome and what you've done with your life since. So, yes, I would welcome you into my family."

Amelia's eyes filled with tears. She grabbed a Kleenex and turned away to compose herself. After a few seconds she said, "You have to say that, of course. It's your job."

"You see how you push me away, Amelia. We got too close for comfort, eh?"

Our time was up. It was pouring outside, and Amelia headed toward the chair on which she had left her raincoat. I reached for it and held it up for her to put it on. She cringed and looked uncomfortable.

"You see?" she said. "You see? That's just what I mean. You're mocking me."

"Farthest thing from my mind, Amelia. It's good you said it, though. It's good to express everything. I like your honesty."

At the door, she turned back to me, saying, "I want a hug."

That was really unusual. I liked her saying it and hugged her, feeling her warmth and bulk.

As she walked down the few stairs leading from my office, I said to her, "You did good work today."

I could hear her first few steps away from me on the gravel path and then, without turning around, she called back over her shoulder, "You did good work too."

Among the issues raised in our session was the odd nostalgia she felt for her old life as an addict. Her explanation that perhaps she was yearning for a life of simplicity recalls the first lines of this book and Heidegger's thought that when one is consumed with everydayness, one turns away from deeper concerns and from incisive self-examination.

My segue into the here-and-now radically shifted the focus of our session. She declined to share her feelings about me and evaded even my question, "Does coming here and seeing me help you stay alive? Keep you away from drugs?" I decided to take the risk of revealing some of my feelings years ago about my therapist.

My modeling helped her take some risks and break new ground. She found the courage to ask an astounding question, a question she had been considering for a very long time: "Would you welcome me as a member of your family?" And, of course, I had to consider this question with the utmost seriousness. I had great respect for her, not only for her climbing out of the pit of heroin addiction but for the way she had lived since then—a moral life dedicated to helping and comforting others. I answered honestly.

And there were no negative repercussions to my answer. I had followed my own guidelines (and my limits) about personal revelation. I knew Amelia very well and was absolutely persuaded that my disclosure would not push her away but would, on the contrary, help her open up.

This was one of many sessions devoted to Amelia's avoidance of intimacy. It was a memorable session, and we often referred back to it. In our subsequent work, Amelia revealed a great deal more about her darker fears. She began to recall many more dreams and memories of the horror of her years on the street. These at first increased her anxiety—an anxiety that heroin used to dissolve—but ultimately allowed her to break down all the inner compartments that had resulted in her being cut off from herself. By the time we terminated, an entire year had gone by without nightmares and the night death panics; and, three years later, I had the pleasure of attending her wedding ceremony.

Self-Disclosure as Modeling

The proper timing and degree of therapist self-disclosure comes with experience. Keep in mind that the purpose of disclosure is always to facilitate the work of therapy. Self-disclosure too early in the course of therapy runs the risk of dismaying or frightening a client who needs more time to ascertain whether the therapy situation is safe. But careful therapist disclosure can serve as an effective model for clients. Therapist disclosure begets patient disclosure.

An example of this therapist disclosure appeared in a recent issue of a psychotherapy journal. The author of the article described an event that occurred twenty-five years before. In a group therapy meeting he had attended, he had noted that the group leader (Hugh Mullen, a well-known therapist) was not only leaning back comfortably but closing his eyes. The letter writer had then asked the leader, "How come you're looking so relaxed, today, Hugh?"

"Because I'm sitting next to a woman," Hugh had immediately responded.

At the time, the writer of the letter had considered the therapist's response to be downright bizarre, and wondered if he were in the wrong group. Gradually, however, he found that this group leader who was unafraid to be up-front with his feelings and fantasies was wonderfully liberating to the group members.

That single comment had true rippling power and exercised such an impact on this man's later career as a therapist that now, twenty-five years later, he felt still so grateful as to write this letter to share the enduring impact of therapist modeling.

DREAMS: THE ROYAL ROAD TO THE HERE-AND-NOW

Dreams are extraordinarily valuable, and it is most unfortunate that many therapists, especially early in their

career, steer clear of them. For one thing, young therapists rarely receive training in dream work. In fact,
many clinical psychology, psychiatry, and counseling
programs make no mention whatsoever of the value of
dreams in therapy. On their own, most young therapists
are daunted by the mysterious nature of the dream, by
the complex and arcane literature on dream symbolism
and interpretation, and by the time-consuming task of
trying to interpret all aspects of a dream. For the most
part, only those therapists who have had intensive personal therapy can fully appreciate the relevance of
dreams.

I try to ease young therapists into working on
dreams by urging them not to worry about interpretation. A fully understood dream? Forget it! It doesn't
exist. Irma's dream, described in Freud's 1900 masterpiece *The Interpretation of Dreams,* the one dream Freud
tried hardest to interpret fully, has been a source of con-
troversy for over a century, and many distinguished
clinicians are still advancing different views of its
meaning.

Think about dreams pragmatically, I tell students.
Think of dreams simply as a bountiful source of information about vanished people, places, and experiences
in the life of a patient. Moreover, death anxiety seeps
into many dreams. Whereas most dreams try to keep
the dreamer asleep, nightmares are dreams in which
naked death anxiety, having broken out of its corral,
terrifies and awakens the dreamer. Other dreams, as I

discussed in Chapter Three, herald an awakening experience; such dreams seem to convey messages from the deep parts of the self that are in touch with the existential facts of life.

Generally, the more fruitful dreams for the therapy process are nightmares, recurrent dreams, or powerful dreams—lucid dreams that stay fixed in memory. If the patient brings several dreams to a session, I generally find that the most recent or the most vivid one offers the most fruitful associations. A strong unconscious force within us strains to conceal dream messages in ingenious ways. Not only do dreams contain obscure symbols and other concealment devices, but they are ethereal: we forget them, and even if we jot down notes of the dream, it is not unusual that we forget to bring our notes into the next therapy session.

So teeming are dreams with representations of unconscious images that Freud called them the *via regia*—the royal road—to the unconscious. But, more important for these pages, dreams are also the via regia to understanding the patient-therapist relationship. I pay particular attention to dreams that contain representations of therapy or the therapist. Generally, as therapy progresses, therapy dreams become more common.

Keep in mind that dreams are almost entirely visual, the mind somehow assigning visual images to abstract concepts. Thus therapy is often depicted visually in such ways as a journey, or repair work being done to one's house, or a trip of discovery in which one finds previously unused, unknown rooms in one's own home. For example, Ellen's dream (described earlier in this chapter) represented her shame in the form of as menstrual blood soaking her clothes in my bathroom, and her distrust of my reliability was represented by my ignoring her, not coming to her aid, and being busy in conversation with others. The following vignette casts light on an important issue for therapists treating patients with death anxiety: the therapist's mortality.

A Dream About the Therapist's Vulnerability: Joan

At the age of fifty, Joan had sought therapy for her persistent fear of death and her night panics. She had been working regularly on these issues for several weeks before this dream interrupted her sleep.

I'm meeting with my therapist (I'm sure he is you, though he doesn't really look quite like you), and I am playing around with some cookies on a large plate. I pick up a couple of cookies and bite off a little corner off each and then break them into crumbs and stir them around with my fingers. Then the therapist picks up the plate and swallows all the crumbs and cookies in one gulp. After a few minutes, he falls on his back and is ill. He then gets sicker and begins to look creepy and grows long green nails. His eyes become ghoulish, and his legs disappear. Larry [her hus-

band] comes in and helps out and comforts him. He is much better at that than I am. I am frozen. I wake up, my heart pounding, and spend the next couple of hours obsessed with death.

"What ideas come into your mind about the dream, Joan?"

"Well, the ghoulish eyes and the legs stir up memories. You remember that I visited my mother a few months ago after her stroke. She was comatose for a week and then, shortly before she died, her eyes partly opened and appeared 'ghoulish.' And my father had a major stroke twenty years ago in which he lost the use of his legs. He spent his last few months in a wheelchair."

"You say you spent a couple of hours obsessing about death when you woke from this dream. Tell me as much as you remember about those hours."

"It's the same stuff I've told you about: the dread of going into blackness forever, and then a great sorrow at my not being there any longer for my family. That's what got me started last night, I think. Before I went to sleep, I was looking at some old photos of my family and realizing that my father, awful as he was to my mother and to us, had an existence too. It was almost as though I was appreciating this for the first time. Maybe looking at my father's photos made me realize that despite everything, he still left some traces of himself, some of them even good traces. Yes, the idea of leaving traces helps. It is comforting to put on my mother's old robe, which I still use, and comforting when I see my daughter drive up in my mother's old Buick."

She continued, "Even though I get something from your discussing all those great thinkers pondering the same question, sometimes those ideas don't really soothe the terror. The mystery is too terrifying: death is such a unknown, such an unknowable darkness."

"Yet you have a taste of death every night when you sleep. Do you know that in Greek mythology, Hypnos and Thanatos, sleep and death, are twin brothers?"

"Perhaps that's why I fight off going to sleep. It's just so barbaric, so incredibly unfair that I have to die."

"Everyone feels that way. I sure do. But that's the deal in existence. It's the deal with us humans. It's the deal with everything that lives—or ever lived."

"It's still so unfair."

"We're all—me, you—a part of nature in all its indifference, a place with no sense of fairness or unfairness."

"I know. I know all this. It's just that I get into this child's state of mind where I'm discovering that truth for the very first time. Each time it seems like the first time. You know I can't talk like this to anyone else. I think your willingness to stay right in there with me is helping me in ways I haven't told you about. I haven't told you, for example, that I'm really carving out some good new spaces for myself at work."

"That's so good to hear, Joan. Let's keep working. Let's go back to the dream," I said. "I didn't stay with you in the dream: I began to vanish. What intuitions do you have about the cookies and what they did to my eyes and legs?"

"Well, I just nibble at the cookie and then stir and play with the crumbs. But you take them and swallow all of them and then look what it does to you. I think the dream reflects my concerns that I am too much for you, that I ask for too much. I nibble away at this scary topic, but you keep plunging in—and not just with me but with your other patients, too. I guess I worry about *your* death, that you will disappear like my parents, like everyone."

"Well, that's going to happen some day, and I know you worry about my being old and worry about my dying and also about the effects on me about your talking about death. But I'm committed to stay in there with you as long as I am physically able. You don't weigh me down, on the contrary, I treasure your trusting me with your innermost thoughts, and I've still got my legs and my eyes are clear."

Joan's concern about dragging her therapist into her despair has some validity: therapists who have not faced their own mortality may indeed find themselves overwhelmed with anxieties about their own death.

The Widow's Nightmare: Carol

Not only do patients worry about overwhelming the therapist, but ultimately, as in Carol's dream, they confront the reality of the limits of what a therapist can do.

I had been seeing Carol, a sixty-year-old widow who had been caring for her elderly mother since her husband's death four years earlier. During our therapy, her mother died, and, feeling too lonely living by herself, Carol had decided to move in with her son and grandchildren in another state. In one of our last few sessions, she reported this dream:

There are four people—me, a guard, a female convict, and you—and we are traveling to a safe place. Then we are in the living room of my son's home—it's safe and has bars on the window. You leave the room just for a moment—perhaps to go to the bathroom—and suddenly a gunshot shatters the window and kills the convict. Then you come back into the room, see her lying there and try to help her. But she dies so quickly you have no time to do anything for her or even to speak to her.

"Feelings in this dream, Carol?"

"It was a nightmare. I woke up frightened, heart pounding away so hard it shook the bed. I couldn't get back to sleep for a long time."

"What comes to mind about the dream?"

"The heavy protection—as much as possible. You were there, and a guard, and bars on the window. Yet despite all that protection, the convict's life still couldn't be protected."

In our ongoing discussion of the dream, she felt that its center, its vital message, was that her death, like the convict's, could not be prevented. She knew that in the dream she was both herself and the convict. Doubling oneself is a common dream phenomenon; in fact, the founder of the gestalt therapy approach, Fritz Perls, considered that every individual or physical object in a dream represents some aspect of the dreamer.

More than anything else, Carol's dream exploded the myth that I would somehow always protect her. There were many intriguing aspects of the dream (for example, her self-image issues were depicted by her doubling herself as a convict or the idea that life with her son evoked an image of a room with bars), but, given the impending termination of therapy, I opted to focus on our relationship, especially on the limits of what I could offer. Carol realized that the dream told her that even if she chose not to move to her son's home and instead stayed connected with me, I still could not protect her from death.

Our last three sessions, spent working on the implications of this insight, not only made it easier for her to terminate treatment with me but also served as an awakening experience. More than ever before, she understood the limits of what she could get from others. Although connection can soften pain, it cannot thwart the most painful aspects of the human condition. She gained strength from this insight, strength that she could carry with her to wherever she chose to live.

Tell Me That Life Is Not Just Shit: Phil

Last, an example of a dream that illuminates aspects of the therapist-patient relationship.

You are a patient very seriously ill in the hospital, and I am your doctor. But instead of taking care of you, I keep asking you, rather insistently, whether you had had a happy life. I wanted you to tell me that life was not just shit.

When I asked Phil, an eighty-year-old man terrified of death, for his ideas about the dream, he immediately commented that he felt as if he were sucking my blood, asking too much of me. The dream portrays this concern with a narrative in which, even though I am ill and he is the doctor, his needs override all else, and he persists in asking for something from me. He is in despair from his ill health and all his dead or disabled friends and wants me to give him hope by telling him that life isn't just shit.

Prompted by the dream, he asked explicitly, "Am I too much of a burden for you?"

"We all have the same burden," I responded, "and your confrontation with the worm at the core [a term for death that he had previously used] is heavy yet enlightening for me. I look forward to our sessions, and my meaning comes from helping you recover your own zest and reconnect with the wisdom that has come from your life experience."

———

I began this book by observing that death anxiety rarely enters the discourse of psychotherapy. Therapists avoid the topic for a number of reasons: they deny the presence or the relevance of death anxiety; they claim that death anxiety is, in fact, anxiety about something else; they may fear igniting their own fears; or they may feel too perplexed or despairing about mortality.

I hope that I have, in these pages, conveyed the necessity and the feasibility of confronting and exploring all fears, even the darkest ones. But we need new tools—a different set of ideas and a different type of therapist-patient relationship. I suggest that we attend to the ideas of great thinkers who have faced death forthrightly and that we build a therapeutic relationship based on the existential facts of life. Everyone is destined to experience both the exhilaration of life and the fear of mortality.

Genuineness, so crucial to effective therapy, takes on a new dimension when a therapist deals honestly with existential issues. We have to abandon those vestiges of a medical model that posits that such patients are suffering from a strange affliction and are in need of a dispassionate, immaculate, perma-sealed healer. We all face the same terror, the wound of mortality, the worm at the core of existence.

Afterword

La Rochefoucauld's maxim, "Le soleil ni la mort ne se peuvent regarder en face," cited on the title page, reflects the folk belief that staring into either the sun or death is noxious. I would recommend staring into the sun to no one, but staring into death is quite another matter. A full unwavering look at death is the message of this book.

History teems with examples of the variegated ways we deny death. Socrates, for example, that staunch champion of the fully examined life, went to his death saying he was grateful to be free of "the foolishness of the body" and was certain he would spend eternity in philosophical converse with like-minded immortals.

The contemporary field of psychotherapy, so dedicated to critical self-exploration, so insistent on excavating the deepest layers of thought, has also shrunk away from examining our fear of death, the paramount and pervasive factor underlying so much of our emotional life.

In my interactions with friends and colleagues during the last two years, I've experienced this evasion firsthand. Ordinarily, when immersed in writing, I am accustomed to long social conversations about my work. Not so with this book. My friends often inquire about my current project. I answer that I am writing about overcoming the terror of death. End of conversation. With only a few exceptions, no one asks a follow-up question, and before long we are on to a different topic.

I believe that we should confront death as we confront other fears. We should contemplate our ultimate end, familiarize ourselves with it, dissect and analyze it, reason with it, and discard terrifying childhood death distortions.

Let's not conclude that death is too painful to bear, that the thought will destroy us, that transiency must be denied lest the truth render life meaningless. Such denial always exacts a price—narrowing our inner life, blurring our vision, blunting our rationality. Ultimately self-deception catches up with us.

Anxiety will always accompany our confrontation with death. I feel it now as I write these words; it is the price we pay for self-awareness. Thus I have deliberately used "terror" in the subtitle (rather than "anxiety") to intimate that raw death terror can be scaled down to everyday manageable anxiety. Staring into the face of death, with guidance, not only quells terror but renders life more poignant, more precious, more vital. Such an approach to death leads to instruction about life. To that end I have focused on how to diminish death terror as well as how to identify and make use of awakening experiences.

I do not intend this to be a somber book. Instead, it is my hope that by grasping, really grasping, our human condition—our finiteness, our brief time in the light—we will come not only to savor the preciousness of each moment and the pleasure of sheer being but to increase our compassion for ourselves and for all other human beings.

Notes

Chapter One: The Mortal Wound

9   *Why not follow the advice:* Adolph Meyer quoted by Jerome Frank, personal communication, 1979.

9   *Hidden and disguised, leaking out in a variety of symptoms:* There is a large, very active field of experimental research on death anxiety (much of it from proponents of "Terror Management Theory"), which demonstrates the ubiquity of death anxiety and its vast influence on self-esteem; on an extraordinarily broad range of personality traits, beliefs, and behavior; and on the tenacity of one's cultural worldview and validated standards. See, for example, Solomon, S., Greenberg, J., and Pyszczynski, T. "Pride and Prejudice: Fear of Death and Social Behavior." *Current Directions in Psychological Science,* 2000, 9(6), 200–204; Pyszczynski, T., Solomon, S., and Greenberg, J. *In the Wake of 9/11: The Psychology of Terror.* Washington, D.C.: American Psychological Association, 2002.

Chapter Two: Recognizing Death Anxiety

12 *The Czech existential novelist Milan Kundera suggests:* Quoted in Roth, P. *Shop Talk: A Writer and His Colleagues and Their Work.* Boston: Houghton Mifflin, 2001, p. 97.

18   *A careful reading of that text:* For more details, see my introduction to a recent edition of Freud, S., and Breuer, J. *Studies on Hysteria* (J. Stracey, ed. and trans.). New York: Basic Books, 2000. (Originally published 1895.)

18   *He offered two reasons:* Freud, S. *Inhibitions, Symptoms, and Anxiety* (J. Strachey, trans.). London: Hogarth Press, 1936. (Originally published 1926.)

18   *Even though Freud wrote poignantly:* Freud, S. "Thoughts for the Time on War and Death: Our Attitudes Toward Death." *Collected Papers of Sigmund Freud.* Vol. 4. London: Hogarth Press, 1925; see also Yalom, I. D. *Existential Psychotherapy.* New York: Basic Books, 1980, pp. 64–69.

19   *His "de-deathification," as Robert Jay Lifton put it, of death:* Lifton, R. J. *The Broken Connection.* New York: Simon & Schuster, 1979.

19   *Indeed, one could argue:* Spiegel, D. "Man as Time-keeper: Philosophical and Psychotherapeutic Issues." *American Journal of Psychoanalysis,* 1981, *41*(5), 14.

20   *Asking a patient to meditate by a grave:* Freud and Breuer, 1895/2000.

28   *The dichotomy she made between ideas and connection:* The necessary synergy of ideas and human connection is the central theme in my novel *The Schopenhauer Cure.* New York: HarperCollins, 2005.

Chapter Three: The Awakening Experience

31   *Instead, it was a form of existential shock therapy:* In the psychiatric literature, such experiences are commonly labeled as "boundary experiences," a translation from

the German existential analytic term *Grenzsituationen,* meaning human boundaries or limits. But the term *boundary* is problematic in contemporary therapy because its primary referent is to the frame—that is, to the boundaries of the therapeutic relationship and the avoidance of other than therapeutic relationships. Hence I propose the term *awakening experience.*

34 *Many reported a diminishment:* Yalom, I. D. *Existential Psychotherapy.* New York: Basic Books, p. 160.

43 *At our next session, I read aloud:* Tolstoy, L. *Anna Karenina.* New York: Modern Library, 2000, p. 168. (Originally published 1877.)

49 *A theme of great importance:* This conclusion is supported by a doctoral research dissertation that confirmed an inverse relationship between death anxiety and life satisfaction—in other words, *the less life satisfaction, the greater the death anxiety.* Godley, C. *Death Anxiety, Defensive Styles, and Life Satisfaction.* Unpublished doctoral dissertation, Colorado State University, 1994.

50 *As did Zorba the Greek:* Kazantzakis, N. *Zorba the Greek.* New York: Simon & Schuster, 1952. (Originally published 1946.)

50 *Sartre, in his autobiography:* Sartre, J.-P. *The Words.* New York: Vintage Books, 1981, p. 198. (Originally published 1964.)

67 *I am in the screened porch:* I described this dream in Yalom, I. D. *Momma and the Meaning of Life.* New York: Basic Books, 1999, p. 138.

Chapter Four: The Power of Ideas

81 *Of the many who have restated this argument:* Nabokov, V. *Speak, Memory.* New York: Putnam, p. 19. (Originally published 1951 as *Conclusive Evidence.*)

87 *In* The Gift of Therapy, *I describe an incident:* Yalom, I. D. *The Gift of Therapy: An Open Letter to a New Generation of Therapists and Their Patients.* New York: HarperCollins, 2001, pp. 187–194.

90 *Freud states the argument:* Freud, S. "On Transience." In J. Strachey (ed. and trans.), *Standard Edition of the Complete Psychological Works of Sigmund Freud.* Vol. 14. London: Hogarth Press, 1955, pp. 304–307. (Originally published 1915.)

93 *Nietzsche, the greatest aphorist of all:* Nietzsche, F. *Human, All Too Human.* Vol. 2. Cambridge: Cambridge University Press, 1986, p. 250. (Originally published 1878.)

93 *In John Gardner's wonderful novel:* Gardner, J. *Grendel.* New York: Vintage Press, 1989, p. 133. (Originally published 1971.)

99 *Try reading them aloud to yourself:* The idea of the "eternal return" thought experiment is fully developed in *Thus Spake Zarathustra,* but this quotation is from an earlier work: Nietzsche, F. *The Gay Science* (W. Kaufman, trans.). New York: Vintage Books, 1974, p. 273. (Originally published 1882.)

104 *Nietzsche claimed two "granite" sentences:* Nietzsche, F. *Thus Spake Zarathustra.* New York: Penguin Books. (Originally published 1891.)

109 *"Some refuse the loan of life":* Rank, O. *Will Therapy and Truth and Reality.* New York: Knopf, 1945, p. 126. (Originally published 1930.)

110 *Otto Rank posited a useful dynamic:* Rank, 1930/1945, pp. 119–133.

110 *This formulation ultimately became the spine:* Becker, E. *Denial of Death.* New York: Free Press, 1973.

112 *For such a person, I find it useful:* Schopenhauer, A. "What a Man Is," "What a Man Has," and "What a Man Represents." *Parerga and Paralipomena.* Vol. 1. Oxford: Oxford University Press, 1974, pp. 323–403. (Originally published 1851.)

Chapter Five: Overcoming Death Terror Through Connection

119 *Confirmation is ubiquitous:* Lambert, C. "The Science of Happiness." *Harvard,* Jan./Feb. 2007. www.harvard magazine.com/on-line/010783.html.

120 *Even the Greek gods fled in fear:* See, for example, Artemis's speech at the end of Euripides' play *Hippolytus.*

120 *As William James wrote:* James, W. *The Principles of Psychology.* Vol. 1. New York: Henry Holt, 1893, p. 293.

122 *Think of the Chinese peasant culture:* Yardley, J. "Dead Bachelors in Remote China Still Find Wives." *New York Times,* Oct. 5, 2006. www.nytimes.com/2006/10/05 /world/asia/05china.html?ex=1180065600&en=3873c0b 06f9d3e41&ei=5070.

125 *A recent survey indicated:* Fox, S., and Fallows, D. *Internet Health Resources.* 2003. http://www.hetinitiative.org

/sub-resources/ehlstudentresearchthorndike.html. Pew Internet & American Life Project. Retrieved Jan. 27, 2007, from http://www.pewinternet.org/PPF/r/95 /report _display.asp.

125 *Research demonstrates that leader-led groups:* Spiegel, D., Bloom, J. R., and Yalom, I. D. "Group Support for Patients with Metastatic Cancer: A Randomized Prospective Outcome Study." *Archives of General Psychiatry,* 1981, *38*(5), 527–533; Spiegel, D., and Glafkides, M. S. "Effects of Group Confrontation with Death and Dying." *International Journal of Group Psychotherapy,* 1983, *33*(4), 433–447.

125 *Recent research also attests:* Lieberman, M. A., and others. "Electronic Support Groups for Breast Carcinoma: A Clinical Trial of Effectiveness." *Cancer,* 2003, *97*(4), 920–925; Lieberman, M. A., and Goldstein, B. "Self-Help Online: An Outcome Evaluation of Breast Cancer Bulletin Boards." *Health Psychology,* 2005, *10*(6), 855–862.

130 *Once, decades ago:* I fictionalized the incident of lying in bed with a dying woman in my novel *Lying on the Couch* (New York: Basic Books, 1996).

132 *As Pascal said:* Pascal, B. *Pensées.* New York: Penguin, 1995. (Originally published 1660.)

132 *In a recent rehearsal of a new play:* http://mednews .stanford.edu/releases/2006/october/deavere.html.

136 *I learned that such displays:* Seligman, M. *Authentic Happiness.* New York: Free Press, 2002.

139 *I applied the same strategy:* Some might consider my approach unfair. After all, when therapists need help and seek therapy, don't they deserve the same caring

and nurturance as other clients? I see many therapists as patients, and I've never fallen prey to this line of thought. When I meet with someone who has much personal expertise, I will always try to put that expertise to work on his or her behalf.

144 *Legions of artists and writers:* Whittier, J. G. "Maud Muller." 1856. http://en.wikiquote.org/wiki/John_Green leaf_Whittier.

Chapter Six: Death Awareness

149 *Nietzsche once commented:* "Gradually it has become clear to me what every great philosophy so far has been: namely the personal confession of its author and a kind of involuntary memoir; also that the moral (or immoral) intentions in every philosophy constituted the real germ of life from which the whole plant has grown." Nietzsche, F. *Beyond Good and Evil.* New York: Vintage Books, 1966, p. 13. (Originally published 1886.)

151 *Buffalo Bill's defunct:* "Buffalo Bill's" Copyright 1923, 1951, (c) 1991 by the Trustees for the E. E. Cummings Trust. Copyright (c) 1976 by George James Firmage, from *Complete Poems: 1904–1962* by E. E. Cummings, edited by George J. Firmage. Used by permission of Liveright Publishing Corporation.

187 *I agree with Thomas Hardy:* Hardy, T. "De Profundis II" (1895–96). *Poems of the Past and the Present.* http://info motions.com/etexts/gutenberg/dirs/etext02/pmpst10 .htm.

196 *Faulkner expressed the same belief:* Quoted in Southall, T. W. *Of Time and Place: Walker Evans and William Christenberry.* San Francisco: Friends of Photography, 1990.

196 *And Paul Theroux said:* Theroux, P. "D Is for Death." In S. Spender (ed.), *Hockney's Alphabet.* New York: Random House, 1991.

196 *This hypnotic therapy technique:* David Spiegel first suggested this split-screen technique to me. See Spiegel, H., and Spiegel, D. *Trance and Treatment: Clinical Uses of Hypnosis.* Washington, D.C.: American Psychiatric Publishing, 2004.

197 *The other half, however, offsets it:* Dawkins, R. *The God Delusion.* Boston: Houghton Mifflin, 2006, p. 361.

198 *If, as Kundera says:* Quoted in Roth, P. *Shop Talk: A Writer and His Colleagues and Their Work.* Boston: Houghton Mifflin, 2002.

Chapter Seven: Addressing Death Anxiety

215 *The therapeutic act is:* Yalom, I. D. *The Gift of Therapy.* New York: HarperCollins, 2002, p. 37.

220 *Moreover, for decades I have sent out:* I discuss this technique in more detail in Yalom, I. D. *The Theory and Practice of Group Psychotherapy.* (5th ed.) New York: Basic Books, 2005, pp. 456–468.

224 *I've discussed the technical approach:* Yalom, 2002, pp. 46–54.

238 *Do not go gentle into that good night:* Thomas, D. "Do Not Go Gentle into That Good Night" (six-line excerpt) by Dylan Thomas, from *The Poems of Dylan Thomas,* copyright © 1952 by Dylan Thomas. Reprinted by permission of New Directions Publishing Corp.

252 *Having recently read a story I had written:* This story
appears in Yalom, I. D. *Love's Executioner.* New York:
Basic Books, 1989.

263 *An example of this therapist disclosure:* Wright, F. "Being
Seen, Moved, Disrupted, and Reconfigured: Group
Leadership from a Relational Perspective." *Internation-
al Journal of Group Psychotherapy,* 2004, *54*(2), 235–250.

About the Author

Irvin D. Yalom is Emeritus Professor of Psychiatry at Stanford University School of Medicine. The author of the definitive textbook *The Theory and Practice of Psychotherapy,* which has sold 700,000 copies in eighteen languages and is now in its fifth edition, he also wrote *Existential Psychotherapy,* a textbook for a course that did not exist at the time. Dr. Yalom has written several trade books for the general reader, including a collection of therapy tales, *Love's Executioner,* which was a *New York Times* best seller; the novels *When Nietzsche Wept,* also a best seller in the United States, Israel, Greece, Turkey, Argentina, Brazil, and Germany (where it sold more than one million copies); *Momma and the Meaning of Life,* a collection of true and fictionalized tales of therapy; *The Gift of Therapy*; and *The Schopenhauer Cure.* Dr. Yalom has an active but part-time private practice in Palo Alto and San Francisco, California.

A READER'S GUIDE
TO
Staring at the Sun

A Reader's Guide to
Staring at the Sun

I rvin Yalom has said that he wrote *Staring at the Sun* as a deeply personal book stemming from his own confrontation with death. "I share the fear of death with every human being: it is our dark shadow from which we are never severed."

Have you too confronted death? Do you share his fear or have such a dark shadow over your life? Do you disagree or agree that such a dark shadow exists for most if not all of us?

After reading *Staring at the Sun,* you might want to ask these questions, either in a group of fellow readers or just on your own. We hope that the following questions to ask the group or yourself alone will help begin a conversation about the issues and questions raised in Dr. Yalom's book.

THE TITLE AND SUBTITLE OF THE BOOK

Do you agree that confronting death is like staring into the sun—something painful, difficult, but necessary if we are to go on living as fully conscious individuals who grasp the true nature of our human condition, our finiteness, our brief time in the light?

Do you understand and agree with the distinction Dr. Yalom makes in the subtitle between overcoming the "terror" of death, but not the fear? Why should we focus on terror only? Is it true that one can never overcome the fear of death?

CHAPTER ONE

Webster's dictionary says an epicure is someone who is devoted to luxurious living and sensuous pleasure. Has Dr. Yalom persuaded you that the Greek philosopher Epicurus has something more valuable to teach us all, and if so, what is it?

Have children from six to puberty ever spoken to you about fearing death? Are they at all curious about death?

Are the teenagers in your world experiencing an upsurge or even an "eruption" of death obsession and anxiety, and if so, how are they expressing it?

You probably know that Sigmund Freud believed that much of our mental problems are a result of repressed sexuality. Irvin Yalom, in contrast, says that much of our anxiety and psychopathology can be traced back to death anxiety. Do you agree? Is that true for you?

CHAPTER TWO

What is your own greatest fear associated with death?
Can you put it in words? Can you visualize it?

   Have you ever had anxiety or fears that you think
are really based on a fear of death?

CHAPTER THREE

Have you ever had an "awakening experience" in your
life, such as a major illness, divorce, loss of a job, retirement, the death of a loved one, a powerful dream, or a
significant reunion?

   How has this kind of experience influenced you or
not in the past? Do you think such an awakening has
the potential to make you appreciate life more or feel
differently about death?

CHAPTER FOUR

Whom do you think you've influenced so far with the
"rippling" in your life? Whom do you think you might
influence with rippling in the future?

Are there any aphorisms, ideas, or sayings—like "That which does not kill me makes me stronger" or "Become who you are"—that you've repeated to yourself in times of stress or when you are experiencing fear of death?

CHAPTER FIVE

Do you agree that being connected intimately to another person can help you deal with the fear of death? Have you ever had such an experience yourself?

Have you ever felt the loneliness of isolation from other people?

Have you ever felt what Dr. Yalom calls existential loneliness, when you realize that no one knows how it is to be you except you, and you understand that death is an end also of the world you constructed throughout your lifetime?

Dr. Yalom cites the Ingmar Bergman film *Cries and Whispers* as a great example of how empathy works. Is there a particular film you've seen that demonstrates human empathy as you have known or would like to know it?

Can you look forward in your life five or ten years and imagine regrets you could have if you keep doing what you're doing now? Can you imagine living in such a way that when you look back a year or five years from now, you will have built no new regrets?

CHAPTER SIX

___

Can you remember your first experience with human death? Who was the first person really close to you who died, and what kind of an experience was that for you?

Have you been to many funerals? Think of a few that have stuck in your memory.

Have you ever had a near-death experience? What was your reaction? How do you feel about it now?

Do you feel that you've fulfilled your childhood dreams? Have you fulfilled your potential?

How do you feel about Dr. Yalom's saying that his work and personal beliefs are rooted in a secular, existential worldview that rejects supernatural beliefs?

Is faith or religion a part of how you cope with death? What do you feel about Dr. Yalom's lack of belief in an afterlife and his statement that the mind (and all that is associated with the mind) ends when the brain stops functioning?

CHAPTER SEVEN

___

Have you ever been or are you now in psychotherapy?

Does your therapist disclose anything about himself or herself? What's this like for you? Have you any desire for more disclosure from your therapist?

Has your therapy ever dealt with problems that, on deeper inspection, turned out to be related to death anxiety?

What does Dr. Yalom's advice that "to become wise you must learn to listen to the wild dogs barking in your cellar" mean to you?

Index